Hamlyn all-colour paperbacks

Geoffrey Hindley

Musical Instruments

illustrated by Ron Geary,
Ralph S. Coventry, Henry Barnett,
Carlo Tora ~~~~~~~~~~~~~~ od

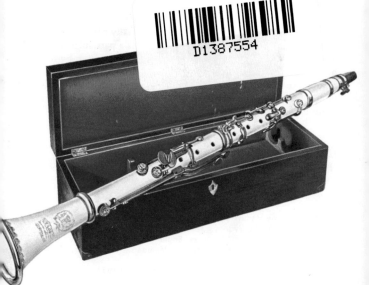

Hamlyn · London
Sun Books · Melbourne

FOREWORD

This book does not pretend to describe all the myriads of musical instruments that the world has seen or even those that are still in use today. However, I hope to have covered all the most familiar instruments to be found in Western European music and also to have introduced the reader to some of the rich variety of instruments of the past, many of which are now being heard again in the concert halls of Europe and America as more and more musicians and listeners explore the splendours of pre-classical music. To complete the survey there is a reasonably full treatment of instruments from non-European cultures.

The plan of the central section is to treat the instruments both in their families, whether woodwind, string, brass or percussion, and in their historical development, so that the reader is able to understand something of the kind of music these instruments served.

The writer admits that he is not a practising musician and has only an amateur's dilettante acquaintance with two or three of the instruments he describes. He has relied in many places on the books listed in the bibliography and acknowledges a particular debt to the scholarly *Musical Instruments through the Ages*, written by members of the Galpin Society and edited by Anthony Baines. Finally, I would like to say that without the magnificent illustrations this book would be very much less interesting and informative, and I am very grateful indeed to the artists.

G.H.

(front cover illustration) Octave spinet. South German, second quarter of the seventeenth century. *(back cover illustration)* French horn

Published by the Hamlyn Publishing Group Limited
London · New York · Sydney · Toronto
Hamlyn House, Feltham, Middlesex, England
In association with Sun Books Pty Ltd., Melbourne

Copyright © The Hamlyn Publishing Group Limited 1971

ISBN 0 600 00294 2
Phototypeset by Filmtype Services Limited, Scarborough
Colour separations by Schwitter Limited, Zurich
Printed in Holland by Smeets, Weert

CONTENTS

PRIMITIVE INSTRUMENTS OF MUSIC

Music has always held a high place in human societies. From the earliest times it has been an essential accompaniment to religious and cult practices, lending dignity to the cathedral service and producing the semi-hypnotic trance of the 'possessed' and the 'oracle'. For some tribes the sound of certain instruments is believed to be the voice of the gods, and the mystery surrounding the divine beings can raise the instruments themselves to the status of sacred objects.

Percussion instruments

Primitive percussion instruments are innumerable. The music of the Aborigines of Australia makes telling use of the simplest means, such as clapper sticks and hand slaps, while the Indian tribes of North America use rattles in ceremonial music. These rattles are of two main types: one used by the priest or *shaman* in rites of healing and dances; the other, usually

(above) Congo wood carving of a drummer
(below) African long drum

4

in the shape of a raven, by the chief on ceremonial occasions. Both types are often elaborately carved.

In many African tribes the royal drums are surrounded by taboos, their manufacture is attended by ritual, and they may even be sacrificed to. There are, of course, many types of drum and they can be played either singly, in pairs, or in large 'batteries'. These may consist of as many as twelve drums of different pitches, each playing different rhythms. For although African music lacks any kind of developed harmonic structure, its rhythmic complexity, resulting from several players performing against one another in conformity with strict conventions, is tremendously powerful.

Drums are also a prime means of communication over long distances. The African drum is well suited for a 'bush telegraph' service; both because of its carrying power and also because it can imitate the tonal nature of the African languages, in which the very pitches of the voice carry meaning. Thus the famous 'talking' drums, carefully tuned and expertly played, do almost literally talk. They are of two main types. The slit drum consists of a hollowed-out log with a slit running down part of its length to form two lips; these are of different thicknesses and give two pitches.

Nigerian hourglass or 'talking' drum, and (right) the instrument being played

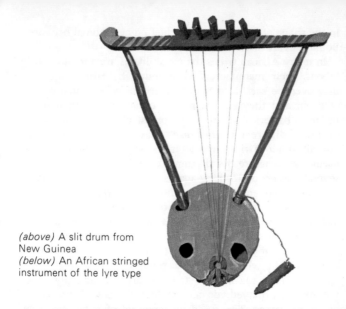

(above) A slit drum from
New Guinea
(below) An African stringed
instrument of the lyre type

More remarkable is the hourglass drum. The heads at either end are connected by thongs and by squeezing these and increasing the tension in the heads, the player can rapidly vary the pitch of the drum through a wide tonal range, so that the drum has the variety of human speech.

Primitive stringed instruments

A primitive type of stringed instrument, virtually indistinguishable from the hunting bow, is still used in parts of Africa and elsewhere. It is possible that the one derived from the other, but it is now thought more likely that the two had independent origins. The pitch of the string can be varied by flexing the bow string while it is being plucked.

But in some cases the player holds one end of the bow in his mouth to serve as a resonating cavity. To alter the pitch of the note he varies the size of the mouth cavity, which emphasizes selected overtones of the vibrating string. Sometimes a gourd is fixed to the bow to increase the resonance still further.

The first lyre was probably formed from an empty turtle or tortoise shell, with two sticks attached to it joined by a cross-piece, and the strings stretched between the cross-piece and the body. The earliest harp may have been made by fixing a bow through the pierced surface of a gourd, used as a sound-box, with the strings stretched between the free end of the bow and running through the body of the gourd to be anchored to the enclosed end of the bow. Finally we should mention the so-called *pluriarc*. This consists of a sound-box to the lower end of which are anchored a number of sticks that project out from the front of the instrument. A string is stretched between the free end of each stick and the top of the sound-box. The different lengths of the strings and the different tensions in their individual sticks or 'necks' produce the various pitches required. The instrument was originally plucked, though it is now sometimes played with a bow. In a sense it may be regarded as the forerunner of the lute and guitar families and, less exactly, of the violin family.

Musical bow and a primitive instrument of the lute type

Primitive wind instruments

After discovering the percussive effects of stick on tree trunk, or hand on body, Man may have made his first musical sound by blowing on a conch shell picked up on the sea shore. With this and the discovery of the possibilities of blowing on hollowed animal horns, early Man had hit on the principle of an air column set in vibration directly by the lips. All the instruments of the horn and trumpet families sprang from this. Primitive trumpets of ancient South America and modern Africa include side-blown varieties with shaped mouthpieces.

The great family of reed instruments may have originated from simple hollow reeds with a loose lip at one end formed by two parallel cuts. The double reed, as used on the modern oboe, was probably discovered later; though an example from about the year 3000 BC was found in the royal tomb at Ur in ancient Sumeria. The flute, in which the air column is vibrated by part of the wall of the instrument itself, was also developed early, and nowhere more fully than in the ancient civilizations of South America. Amongst certain tribes there, deep sounding flutes, played by initiates or priests in parts of

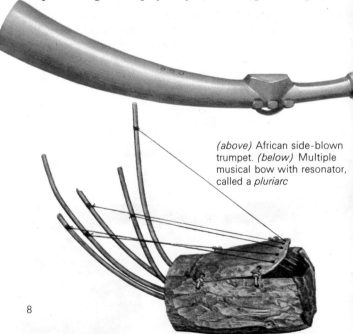

(above) African side-blown trumpet. *(below)* Multiple musical bow with resonator, called a *pluriarc*

the forest remote from the village, are believed to be the voice of the gods, and only men are allowed to look on them. Elsewhere the bull-roarer is held in similar respect. It consists simply of a piece of shaped wood attached to a thong or cord. When it is whirled round the head, the resultant turbulence set up in the air produces a deep harsh roar.

But the most fascinating of all these early wind instruments must surely be the Australian Aboriginal *didjeridoo*. It is again simple, consisting merely of a wooden tube sounded by being blown across one end so that the player's breath vibrates the opposite side of the rim. Only two notes are available; the fundamental note of the whole air column and another about one-tenth above it. But these two notes are enough for the best performers who, displaying considerable virtuosity, use them to set up elaborate and throbbing counter rhythms.

(above) Types of flute from
Venezuela
(below) Bolivian peasant
playing a conch shell

MUSIC IN THE ANCIENT WORLD

The peoples of the ancient Mediterranean world had a deep semi-religious respect for the power of music. The Hebrews' love of music is clear from the many references to musicians and instruments in the Old Testament. David, the most famous Jewish king, was a renowned singer and player on the harp (the Hebrew *kinnōr* should in fact be translated as lyre). The Greek god Apollo, whose emblem was the lyre, was so jealous of his skill as a musician, that when the Muses had awarded him the victory in a flute-playing contest with the satyr Marsyas, he flayed him alive for presuming to challenge a god. Most famous of all is Orpheus who '. . . made trees, and the mountain tops that freeze, Bow themselves when he did sing', and whose skill on the lyre charmed the god of Death himself.

Early stringed instruments

One of the oldest models of a stringed instrument is carried by the little statuette of a harpist illustrated on this page. Despite the stylization, we can tell that this type of instrument, used in the Greek Cycladic islands about 2500 BC, has a rigid frame, unlike the bowed harp being played by the Egyptian girl musician. A harp was found in the royal tomb at Ur, and this kind of instrument was used for ceremonial and social occasions in the civilizations of Sumeria and Egypt. The Egyptians also had a long-necked lute with two strings and an oblong body, and a six-stringed lyre played with a plectrum. But for more than two thousand years it was the harp that enjoyed pride of place among the stringed instruments of ancient Egypt, where it was played by royal ladies and bards, who sang songs of love and of the legends of the gods. And from Egypt, too, we first hear of blind musicians, whose virtuosity has astonished their listeners from the time of Homer to the present day.

Homer himself probably accompanied his performances of his great epics on an early form of the *cithara*, the bardic

(left) Cycladic figure of a harp player, about 1100 BC
(right) A harpist from an Egyptian wall painting

instrument *par excellence* of Classical Greece. It was a large instrument held against the player's body and kept in position by a sling passing round the left wrist and the body of the instrument. The strings were plucked with a heavy plectrum, probably in a sweeping motion, while the fingers of the left hand damped the unwanted strings.

Early wind and percussion instruments

Although used in temple rituals in ancient Sumeria, the wind instruments of the ancient world seem to have remained closer to their humble origins in the shepherd's pipe, essential for keeping the flock together, than the noble stringed instruments. This may well have been because the mode of playing, particularly of the reed instruments, may have been considered unbecoming to gentlefolk. To this day in Africa, and in some folk traditions of Europe, the wind player develops grotesquely distended cheeks to serve as a wind reservoir.

The Egyptians of pre-dynastic times used a type of three-holed flute, but the Classical world knew a variety of other flutes, including the panpipes (a group of short rim-blown flutes bound together, each providing a separate note). But it seems that the most thrilling wind instrument of the Greeks was the *aulos*. This was sounded by a double reed (as is the modern oboe) and must have had a raucous sound, since vase

Roman street musicians

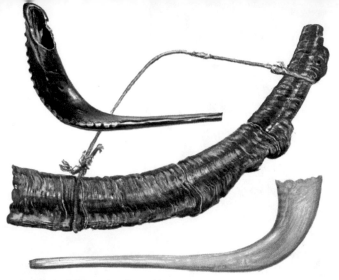

Hebrew *shofarim* made of rams' horns

paintings show it being used to lead troops into battle. It was commonly played in pairs by a single player.

The elaborate Roman *hydraulos* organ consisted of ranks of pipes sounded by wind from a bellows, and controlled from a keyboard by sliders; it had three or four ranks of different kinds of pipes. The name derives from the fact that a steady air pressure was kept up by water pressure. The wind chest was partly filled with water and connected to an outer reservoir; air entering the wind chest forced the water level down, and that in the outer reservoir up; the water level tended to stabilize itself and the wind pressure was maintained.

Numerous types of trumpet and horn were used in ancient civilizations. The Romans had long war trumpets; one straight, and one curving in a huge circle round the player's body. The *shofar*, used in the temple music of Jerusalem, and still heard in the modern synagogue, was a simple ram's horn. Among ancient percussion instruments was the *sistrum*, a hoop-shaped iron frame with three or four iron bars slotted through holes in the sides. As can be seen from the illustration, small cymbals and tambourines were also used as, of course, were various types of drum.

A Chinese *pï p'a* player. *(opposite)* A Chinese 'moon' guitar

MUSICAL INSTRUMENTS OF THE EAST

Chinese music

At first hearing, Oriental music is bound to seem difficult to Western audiences, but one aspect which can almost immediately be appreciated is the fascinating new world of tone colours opened up by the instruments. But first, a few comments on some fundamental concepts of Chinese music which provided the basis for music throughout the Orient.

Chinese classical music was based on a system of five note scales derived from twelve fundamental notes called *lu*. These were arrived at by elaborate calculations which established the absolute pitch of a foundation note called the *huang-chung* or 'yellow bell'. The pitch was given by the length of an open pipe of a carefully defined length. From the earliest times music held a central place in Chinese life – in the early primitive festivals of the agricultural year, in the ceremonial of the Imperial court; and in religious ritual. It was believed that the function of music was to imitate and sustain the mystic harmony between the worlds of Heaven and Earth.

Melody and timbre were the main elements of Chinese music. Large orchestras, sometimes of more than one hundred instruments, were used. But the most highly respected music was that of the *ch'in* zither, from which the Japanese *koto* was possibly derived. It consists of a six-foot long board, slightly convex, with two short legs at one end, the other end being supported on the knee of the cross-legged player. There are seven silken strings, equal in length but varying in thickness, calculated according to acoustic principles to give a sequence of intervals of fourths and fifths on the six open strings. The seventh string, which supplies the melody, is stopped against thirteen mother-of-pearl discs, which serve as frets. The *ch'in*, which may have been perfected in the time of Confucius, remained the instrument of the philosopher and intellectual.

A somewhat more popular instrument was the *p'i p'a*. This was a short-necked lute with a flat, shallow body and a fretted neck. It was much used for song accompaniments and in the T'ang dynasty was developed as a solo instrument. Composers for the *p'i p'a* often wrote music in programmatic style imitating such effects as the sound of battle. Another interesting plucked instrument is the strange and beautiful so-called 'moon' guitar.

The Chinese had instruments from all the familiar categories; wind, string, and percussion, but classified them according to the material used to build them, since the musical sound produced was believed to be an important attribute of the material producing it. There were numerous categories; the silk instruments included the *ch'in*; the metal instruments included various types of bell chimes and gongs and the stone instruments included the chime or tuned stone resonators – one of the most important instruments of Chinese music. The bamboo class embraced many of the wind instruments, notably the shawms; loud double reed instruments suitable for outdoor music. The percussion section was composed of instruments in the wood and skin categories, while the most original of all Chinese instruments, the *sheng* mouth organ, was classed with the gourd instruments. It did not become known in the West until the late eighteenth century when it probably inspired the research that led to the family of metal reed instruments, such as the accordion. A Vietnamese derivative of the *sheng* is illustrated. The classical Chinese instrument consisted of a cluster of seventeen pipes of bamboo set upright in a gourd; fourteen of the pipes were provided with free metal reeds set in the gourd wind chest (the other pipes being dummies to preserve the symmetry of the instrument which was thought to represent the phoenix). The speaking pipes have small holes at their bases which have to be closed by the fingers of the player for the reeds to speak. These are set in vibration by the exhaltation and inhalation of the player blowing and sucking through a side pipe, and the instrument provides a texture of slowly changing cords.

Vietnamese peasant playing a primitive type of *sheng*

Indian music

According to Hindu tradition, the art of music was taught to men by the agency of the god Brahma, and it is probable that the principles of classical Indian music derived, originally, from the sung recitation of the Vedic hymns to the deities. From these semi-legendary traditions developed a body of theoretical treatises. The most ancient, the Natya-Shastra, deals with rhythm and ways of developing a melody, and is much concerned with the dance, considered to be a subdivision of music. A much later treatise, dating from the thirteenth century, contains models of composition which influenced the classical oral tradition.

Acoustic theory divides the octave into some twenty intervals, and from these the *rāgs* are formed; there are very many, but each has generally seven notes. Thus the *rāg* is a type of scale but each one is felt to have almost metaphysical allusions and may be related to a particular time of the day or have other – to the Western mind – extra-musical connotations. For the Indian, how-

An Indian *vīnā*

ever, the mood of the *rāg* can also be expressed in both literature and painting. The skill of the musician, working within strict conventions, which nevertheless allow for imaginative improvisations on his part, lies in his ability to express this mood by exploiting the nuances of pitch and types of ornament allowed so as to present the fullest range of relationships between the notes of the chosen *rāg*. The mainsprings of Indian music are rhythm and the sequence of intervals. Each note of the melody is heard in relationship to the *sa* (or 'key' note). This is sounded throughout the music, either by a special drone instrument, or on drone strings fitted to the stringed instruments.

The classic instrument is the *vīnā*. It normally has seven strings, of which four, plucked with plectra attached to the middle fingers of the right hand and stopped against twenty-four raised metal frets, provide the melody. The remaining three are drone strings plucked by the thumb and little finger. The instrument usually has two gourd resonators attached to the broad wooden neck.

More popular in the north of India is the *sitār*, in appearance similar to a long-necked lute, but in fact probably derived from the zither-like *vīnā*, only less technically demanding. The body is formed by a hollow gourd covered with a wooden belly. A long neck, about three inches broad, carries between

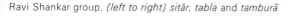

Ravi Shankar group, *(left to right) sitār, tabla* and *tamburā*

Diagram of a drum head of one
of the *tabla* pair, showing hard,
high-pitched central section

sixteen and twenty movable frets that arch over the neck.
There are now usually seven strings, only one of which provides the melody, the others serving as drone accompaniment.
Many *sitārs* also have upwards of thirteen sympathetic strings
which can be tuned to emphasize chosen notes of the *rāg*. The
arched frets enable the player to *bend* notes by pulling the
string out of its direct alignment.

Another important stringed instrument of northern India is
the *sarōd*; it has a heavy wooden body covered with a
parchment belly, a comparatively short neck and a metal
fingerboard without frets. With the numerous strings under
his fingers, the *sarōd* player frequently has to make fine
tuning adjustments and to assist him in this he is accompanied
by a simple four-stringed long-necked lute, the *tamburā*,
which quietly sounds certain of the basic notes of the *rāg*
throughout the performance.

To *sitār* and *tamburā* is added the immensely important
tabla, to form the familiar ensemble of classical instrumental
music. The *tabla* is a set of two small kettledrums, played with

the fingers and heel of the hand; the lower pitched drum, played by the left hand, is about fifteen inches in diameter, the right hand drum about twelve inches. Each consists of copper or brass 'kettle' with a vellum head tensioned by thongs secured at the bottom of the drum. On the smaller drum a number of short wooden cylinders between the thongs and the bulging kettle, allow the player to effect fine tuning by moving them either towards or away from the shoulder of the bulge. In the centre of each head is a small disc of specially treated vellum, which gives a very high pitched 'toc' when struck. Together with the variety of percussive strokes employed, this gives the drummer a fair range of different tone colours with which to articulate the immensely complicated rhythms that he builds upon the basic formulae known as *tals*; these may stretch over as many as sixteen measures.

Indian music also has a number of wind instruments among which the unkeyed *bansurī* flute and the reed instrument known as the *shannāi* (related to the European shawm) have both found outstanding modern virtuosi.

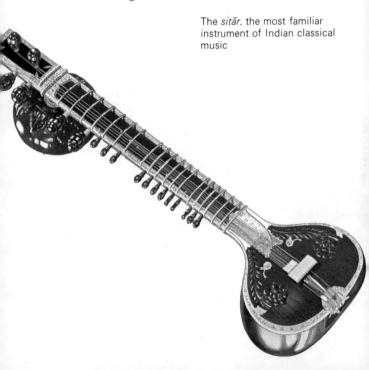

The *sitār*, the most familiar instrument of Indian classical music

Japanese music

Whereas Indian music owes little to any other major culture, that of Japan is heavily indebted to the Chinese tradition and also, through Buddhism, to India. Indeed the classical *Bugaku* music of the Japanese Imperial orchestra of today represents, in fossilized and adapted form, the music heard at the Courts of sixth-century Indian and Chinese rulers. Following the Chinese example, Japan during the eighth-century Nara period founded an Imperial office of music, and not only theory but also instruments were adopted from the mainland. The *biwa*, a short-necked lute, is derived from the *p'i p'a*; the *sho* mouth-organ from the Chinese *sheng*, and even the *samisen*, one of the most characteristic of Japanese instruments, had its first form in China. The case of the *koto* zither is less straight-forward since it had two forms, one of which was considered to be of purely Japanese origin. In any case, the *koto* that became the object of intellectual cultivation during the

A Japanese *koto* with plectra

A Japanese musician playing
the *samisen*

seventeenth century was more complicated in structure than
the *ch'in*. Over the six-foot long convex board that forms
the body are stretched thirteen waxed silken strings that
pass over movable bridges; these can be moved with one hand
as the other plucks them with plectra which are attached to the
fingers.

In addition to the *Gagaku* or 'elegant' music of the Court
there were other styles, some associated with the various
types of Japanese theatre. Here the most important instrument
is the *samisen*. First introduced into the orchestras of the more
popular *Kabuki*, it was later adopted even by the highly
stylized *No* theatre. The *samisen* is a three-stringed instrument
with a long neck and a deep square body of wood covered
with cat-skin. It is without frets, and is plucked with a large
axe-shaped plectrum, with a heavy, almost percussive, stroke.

23

Indonesian music

The Chinese influence, so strong in south-east Asia, was of little importance in Indonesia. Here the traditions of Indian Hinduism and of Islam had a far greater impact. A spike fiddle, related to the Arabic *rabāb*, is used in the *gamelan* orchestras of Java and Bali, though their unique sound is produced by fixed-note percussion instruments of the xylophone type. The characteristic sonorities of the *gamelan* reflect the ringing sounds of bamboo on stone, which are commonly heard in the rice fields throughout south-east Asia and Indonesia.

The principal *gamelan* instruments are the *saron*, a metallophone with bronze keys; the *bonang*, a chime of different sized gongs; various types of gongs used individually (such as the *gong ageng*, illustrated here), some swinging freely but most, like those of the *bonang*, attached at the opposite sides of their perimeters with cords or thongs to a wooden frame; a two-headed leather drum; metal drums and many types of wooden keyed xylophones. In addition to these there are also a small number of stringed instruments of foreign origin, and flutes, of which the Javanese ribbon flute (one in which a characteristic 'buzz' is given to the sound by a thin ribbon stretched over a special hole), is the most important. The *gamelan* orchestra is, even now, common in the Indonesian islands. As may be expected, differences are found not only dependeing on the type of music being played, but also on the locality. The most important distinctions are between the main groups of Bali and Java. *Gamelan* music has three main elements. At the centre of the piece is the main 'theme', sounded by the *saron* in long notes punctuated by gong strokes, and the sound of the *kendang* drum, that indicates the basic rhythm. The main theme thus defined is elaborated by a higher pitched group of instruments, such as the *bonang* and a xylophone with bamboo resonators called the *gender*. Above this a still freer and more rapid pattern is played by the flutes and strings. The total effect of *gamelan* music has impressed many European composers since Debussy was first thrilled by it at the Paris Exhibition of 1889.

Indonesian *gong ageng, gender* and *saron demung* xylophone

Arabic music

The music of the Arab world, like that of India, is based on a system of modes, and uses a system of intervals which includes one that is greater than the semi-tone, yet less than the tone. Classical Arabic music arose after the great movements of conquest in the seventh century; prior to the sophisticated culture of Islam, the Arab nomads had used various songs, some of which had had a rudimentary accompaniment provided by lute, flute and frame drum. Under the Islamic period the lute continued to be a major instrument, and it was from the Arab world that it came to Europe in its original unfretted form and played with a plectrum, as it still is today in Arab countries. As Arab conquests extended to Persia, the lute became still more important and its music was affected by the 'romanticizing' influence of the ancient and 'decadent' civilization. Mahomet himself, aware of what he regarded as the dangers of sophistication in the arts, had tried to limit 'art' music to the service of religion, in which the

A musician playing the Arab lute — note the absence of frets

voice of the *muezzin* from the minaret had been supreme. But it has been pointed out that the vocalizations of the *muezzin* were little different from those of the professional singers who won immense reputations for themselves at the secular courts. Furthermore, as Arab culture progressed in sophistication, the searching minds of the theorists made of the lute itself a scientific instrument of theoretical speculation with which to give body to the theoretical speculations sparked off by the Arab discovery and extension of Greek acoustic theory. In addition to the lute there was the bowed *rabāb* (spike fiddle) and the *naqqāra*, (early small kettledrums). Arabic music uses a number of other stringed instruments, drums, and wind instruments such as the double-reed *zurnā*, equivalent to the European shawm.

A zither

INSTRUMENTS OF EUROPEAN FOLK MUSIC

All the great traditions described in the foregoing pages share certain common features. First, their music is primarily melodic; secondly, although numerous conventions govern the mode of the performance, the musician is allowed considerable scope for improvisation and is expected to use it imaginatively; thirdly, the survival of the tradition depends on oral transmission rather than notated records. All these features are to be found in European folk music. Since the Middle Ages there has been more or less active cross fertilization between 'folk' music and that of 'high' culture. Instruments which were once used both by the musicians of the Court and by the common people have lingered on exclusively as folk instruments, and there are also instances of old Court dances fossilized in surviving folk airs.

In many parts of Europe and America folk musicians make use of instruments such as the fiddle and the accordion, the double bass, or the guitar, which are commonly used in other types of music.

The music of Mediterranean Europe has been heavily coloured by the influence of Islam; and in Eastern European countries, such as Greece and the Balkans, by the long years of Turkish occupation. The lute and various types of drum are derived from the Arab world, and the numerous shawms throughout the region have Arab or Turkish equivalents such as the *zurla*. However, an interesting exception to this is the Aegean fiddle known as the *lyra*. This was probably the ancestor of the medieval *rebec* – although the word is derived from the Arabic *rabāb*, there is in fact no connexion between them since the Arabic instrument is a spike fiddle and the *rebec* is not. The Aegean fiddle is still played by street and folk musicians in Greece and is often used by bards and singers to accompany their songs. It is held vertically on the knee with the bow palm upwards. Perhaps the best-known of modern Greek folk instruments is the *buzuki*, a long-necked type of lute with frets. It has been suggested that it is distantly related, through Turkish descent, to the *tamburā* of India.

John Leach playing the Hungarian *zimbalom*

The unique and delightful sound of the *buzuki*-bands of Greece is a lively reminder of the spirit and resilience of that much oppressed people.

In the Balkans also, the long centuries of Turkish rule have left their mark, while further to the north in such lands as the Ukraine, the influence of Asia is felt. Among the most characteristic instruments of this wide central region are the *zimbalom* or *cimbalom* of Hungary and the numerous types of zither found in Austria and the Tyrol. The *cimbalom* is as a backing to the violin and double bass, and is also played in Greece, Rumania, Czechoslovakia and other Central European countries. It consists of a trapezoid-shaped body over which are stretched a number of strings that provide the full melodic range, and are not stopped but struck with light wooden hammers. The Austrian zither, on the other hand – an elaborated version of one of the most ancient principles of stringed instruments – has four melody strings stopped against a fingerboard on the long side of the rectangular body near to the player, and

A *fujara* flute from the Balkans

a number of accompaniment strings, sometimes as many as thirty-seven. In addition to these and other stringed instruments, the Central European region has a wide variety of flutes: among them the *fujara* whistle flute, the rim-blown *kaval* of the Balkans and the panpipes.

Tradition, which in the remoter regions is still vigorous, has its roots in a distant past; the bardic singers of the Balkan countries of today are most probably heirs to a technique that stretches back to the time of Homer. Yet not everything is serious. The village band pictured here is on its way to a wedding, which will be anything but serious. The progress of such travelling bands was once such a common sight, that Rumanian musicians evolved a type of composition, gradually swelling in volume and then dying away again, to represent the band's riotous progress past the bystanders.

A Rumanian village band

MUSICAL INSTRUMENTS IN THE MIDDLE AGES

Medieval stringed instruments

Very few instruments have survived from the earliest centuries, and we are obliged to rely on evidence taken from paintings and sculptures. Clearly instruments were used both in the Church and in the entertainments of lay society, but it is not until about the ninth and tenth centuries that speculation is replaced by any reliable evidence. We know that by the tenth century the organ was to be found in many European churches, probably brought back to Europe from the Byzantine Empire, where it seems to have been in continual use since Classical times. On the great feast days of the Church, the plainsong of the service, normally unaccompanied, came to be reinforced with the pipes of massive organs.

Whereas some medieval stringed instruments originated outside Europe, the ancient Welsh bowed lyre, called the *crwth*, may have Celtic origins. In its earliest form it was

(left) Classic shape of the Celtic harp and *(right)* a Welsh *crwth*

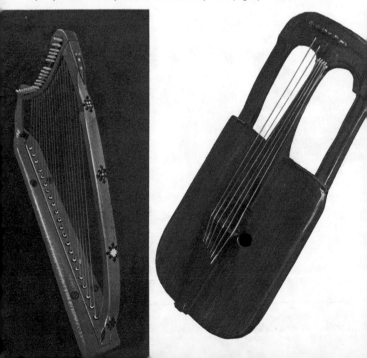

probably plucked, but it seems to have been fitted with a fingerboard during the twelfth century, and from that time was played with a bow.

The three-membered frame of the medieval harp distinguishes it from the more ancient harps of the Middle East. Its structure is as follows: the straight body, or sound-box, held by the player against his body has the strings anchored down its centre. They are tensioned between it and the neck, whose elegant shape – known as the 'harmonic curve' – is determined by the need to ensure that the strings, while varying in length so as to give the required notes, maintain, as far as possible, an equal tension. The neck also carries the tuning pins, which in the Middle Ages were turned with the aid of a large 'T'-shaped key, as can be seen from illuminated manuscripts. The distinguishing feature of the medieval harp, and that still retained in the Irish harp, occurs in the third member of the frame – the gently curving frontal pillar. In later harps this pillar, the function of which

A Renaissance harp

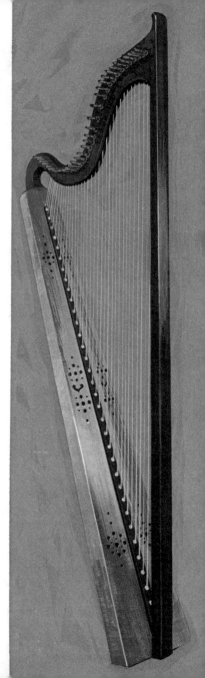

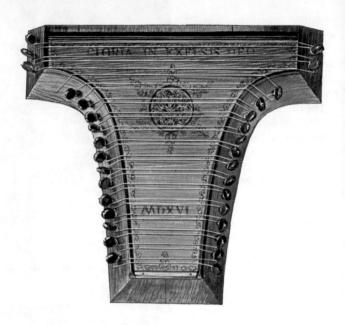

A medieval French psaltery

was to support the neck against the pull of the strings, was straight.

The medieval harp, used by bards to accompany epic recitals, was comparatively small. Some were as little as two feet in height, and only during the Renaissance did a height of four feet become at all common. Until the Renaissance the diatonic range of the instrument (a scale represented by the white notes of the piano only) presented few problems, but as music became more complicated, experiments, of which the first seems to have been in the earlier years of the seventeenth century, were made to fit new strings to provide the missing chromatic notes. The problem that remained for another two centuries was essentially to bring the large number of strings required easily under the hands of the player.

The harp was not the only plucked instrument of the Middle

Ages. Lyres were also used, and in the later Middle Ages the psaltery – probably developed in the Middle East during the ninth century. Like the harp it consisted of a group of unstopped tuned strings, but instead of being strung on a frame, these were stretched across a flat, often trapezoid-shaped, sound-box fitted with soundholes.

At that time the instrument had the general appearance of a zither, with the difference that on a true zither the strings providing the melody are stopped against a fingerboard. Held either flat against the chest with one edge resting on the player's knee, or laid on a table, the psaltery was played with two quills, one in each hand. Like the harp, the psaltery was incapable of a chromatic compass, and gradually gave place not only to the harpsichord itself, but also to the lute and the ancestors of the modern guitar.

One of these was the medieval gittern. A fine fourteenth-century example in the British Museum, although greatly modified by a later hand, gives some idea of the instrument which remained

The Spanish *vihuela*

popular in northern Europe well into the sixteenth century. It had a fretted fingerboard, four courses of strings and was played with a plectrum.

The *vihuela* was very similar to the modern guitar, except that it had a much less marked waist. In the fifteenth and sixteenth centuries, Spain developed a school of composition for it that demanded outstanding virtuosity from the performers. The only distinction between the *vihuela* and the early guitar was simply a matter of stringing; the former having six courses, the latter, for which Renaissance composers also wrote – though less demanding and florid music – having only four. In addition to the plucked instrument here described, there was also a bowed *vihuela* that may have been the forerunner of the viol or violin families.

Medieval bowed instruments

The bowed instruments, as a group, present scholars with an intriguing mystery. There is no record of them anywhere in the civilized world before the ninth century, yet by the

Angel playing the one-stringed *'tromba marina'*, from a painting by Hans Memlinc

(above) Medieval *vielle* and *(below)* medieval *rebec*

end of the tenth they are to be found throughout Europe and Asia. Nor is it known whether the principle of the bow derives from any ancient practice in primitive music. All the known bowed instruments can be traced ultimately to that enigmatic period of the eighth and ninth centuries A.D.

The Chinese fiddle has two strings and no fingerboard, while other early bowed instruments have only one string. This, taken in conjunction with the fact that medieval fiddling technique made use extensively of the 'bourdon' or drone, tempts the suggestion that the inventors of bowed instruments, whoever they may have been, intended them not primarily as melodic, but rather as drone instruments. The Western European *rebec* derived probably from the Aegean fiddle, but by the thirteenth century another type, the *viola* or *vielle*, with oval or slightly waisted body and flat peg disc, had made its appearance. Medieval illustrations of both these types show them held downwards with the bowing hand palm upwards, or held against the chest, or even under the chin with the bowing palm held downwards.

One of the strangest applications of the bow was to the ancient monochord, a simple one-stringed zither with a movable bridge, originally devised, it is thought, as an aid to acoustic theoretical analysis. The result of this improbable union was a bowed chordophone called the trumpet marine or *tromba marina*, also the 'nun's trumpet' or *Marientrompete*. At its most fully developed, it consisted of a single gut string stretched over a long pyramidal body and passing over a loose bridge, one leg of which was free to vibrate against a metal plate giving a buzzing sound; this may account for the 'trumpet'.

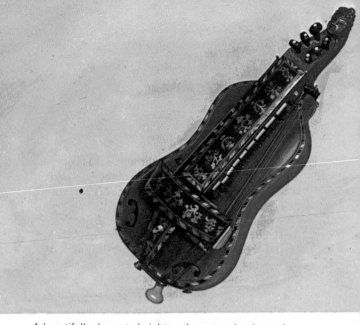

A beautifully decorated eighteenth-century hurdy-gurdy

Medieval drone instruments

Only slightly more familiar to the modern music lover – but considerably more important in early music – was the hurdy-gurdy, which is still used in folk music today. This existed in two versions, one bowed, the other using a resined wooden wheel to vibrate the strings. Apart from these variants the basic elements of the hurdy-gurdy were the two outer drone strings and the fact that the melody strings were stopped, not with the fingers of the performer, but by wooden sliders moving in a casing over the strings, as shown in the illustration.

Known also as the *symphonie*, the *vielle* and the *chifonie*, it long occupied an honourable place in early medieval 'art' music. A large model was known that required two players; one like an organ blower to turn the handle, the other to stop the strings. Much later, the principle of the wheel cymbals was applied to a keyboard mechanism to produce the strange instrument called a *Geigenwerk* illustrated opposite.

The high standing of the hurdy-gurdy during the early Middle Ages and its subsequent decline in social status to that of a folk instrument should be compared to a similar curve in the prestige of the pipe and tabor, to be described later, and the bagpipe. In both cases, illustrations from the medieval and early Renaissance periods show the instruments being used to accompany the dances of courtly society. Of course, many of these dances themselves originated in the world of the peasantry and were taken over by their social superiors, at first in a more or less unexpurgated state, though they became increasingly refined. Perhaps it is this pattern that in part explains the lost caste of the lusty peasant instruments in a later age, when during the pursuit of rusticity and artificial delights of Arcadia these folk instruments enjoyed a new and somewhat precious vogue. The elaborately decorated hurdy-gurdy illustrated on the previous page, and the

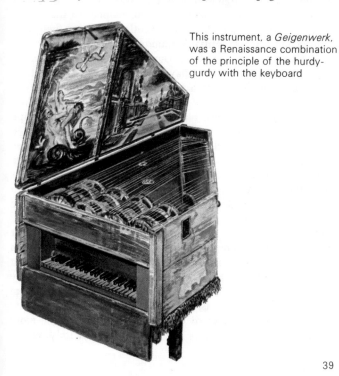

This instrument, a *Geigenwerk*, was a Renaissance combination of the principle of the hurdy-gurdy with the keyboard

delicate little *musette* shown here, vividly picture this aspect of their history.

It will be noticed that all three instruments referred to enabled a single player to buttress a melodic line and to be heard above the bustle of the dance, in a way impossible for performers on simple pipes. But as ensemble-playing of instruments and instrumental polyphonic music became increasingly common, so the popularity of these 'one-man-band' ensembles declined. Despite its long naturalization on European soil, it is almost certain that the bagpipe had its origin in the Middle East, probably in the great cities of the region, some time in the first century BC or the first century AD. It was certainly known to the Romans, and may even have been one of the instruments of that self-satisfied and certainly publicly acclaimed musical virtuoso, the Emperor Nero. But the mode of its adoption in medieval Europe is unknown. However, by the High Middle Ages, it was known throughout the Continent, and regional models developed, so that today Poland, Italy, Brittany, Spain and Scotland all have their own unique and easily identifiable sounds.

The essential feature of the bagpipe, which affects its mode of performance and may have led to its development, is the wind reservoir, which is made from an animal bladder and is held under the arm of the player, who keeps it filled with air from his lungs, blown through a narrow blowpipe with a one-way leather valve. The melody is provided by a pipe called the chanter and the drone bass by much longer pipes which are tuned to the octave and the fifth below the chanter keynote. Originally there was only one such drone pipe, but from the later Middle Ages many styles of bagpipe had two drones, while the Scottish and Breton pipes now have three drones. At the base of all the speaking pipes are single reeds. In the Polish bagpipe and those of other countries, the chanter has a cylindrical bore, and the wilder tones of the Scottish highland pipes are partly to be accounted for by the fact that in these, the chanter has a conical bore. A further contributory factor to the familiar sound of the pipes is derived from the fact that the scale is, in certain of its degrees, not quite in tune with the standard diatonic scale. Some of the more interesting varieties of pipe are the *zampogna* of Italy, which

(above) The bagpiper, from a well-known engraving by Dürer. *(below)* An eighteenth-century *musette* from *Two Studies of a Bagpiper* by Watteau

has two chanters, one for each hand, and the Breton *biniou* in which the chanter and drones are played by two performers. In others, such as the Northumbrian shuttle pipe and the Galway pipe, the air is supplied not by the player, who may, if he so wishes, smoke the other kind of pipe while he plays, but by a bellows tucked under one arm. This expedient was adopted for the 'society' *musette,* illustrated on the previous page, no doubt because it was felt to be not quite elegant for the aristocracy to have to suffer the distended cheeks of the peasantry.

For the English-speaking peoples the bagpipe is associated, above all, with the skirl of the Highland pipe bands which, like those of the Breton regiments, have so often led their troops into battle. But among the numerous forms of the instrument that have been developed in the different regions of Europe, from the Middle Ages to the present day, we should remember that the bagpipes have been both raucous and dulcet in their tones. No doubt the instrument played

A Highland piper in full dress

by Chaucer's bawdy Miller was sufficiently loud, but it was essentially the same as the gentle *musette* that delighted the ears of the Court of Marie Antoinette.

Above all, whatever their means of wind supply, and however sweet their voice, all the members of the bagpipe family are subject to one limiting technical factor. Since the wind supply is continuous and since the player has no direct contact with the reeds that make the chanter speak, he is obliged to make use of a number of ornamental figures to give articulation to the melody. In some cases the fundamental note of the chanter, often the octave above the drone, is sounded between notes of the melody to separate them from one another; sometimes notes above the melody note may be struck for the same purpose; but always the piper must find some such means of giving his melody shape.

Hungarian bock pipes

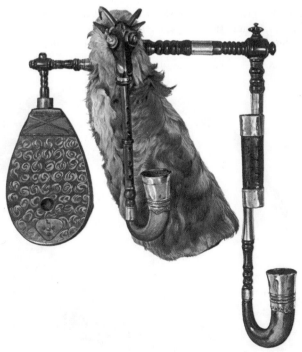

Medieval drums and trumpets

Among the other wind instruments used during the Middle Ages there were various types of flute including, towards the end of the period, the transverse flute and, from as early as the fourteenth century, the recorder. There were also reed instruments, among them members of the double-reed shawm family, which the Renaissance was to develop more fully; a type of the panpipes called the *fretel* and a number of instruments that provided the ancestors of the modern brass section of the orchestra. From an early period, of course, the brass had been used in war; the Roman war trumpet has been mentioned, and the Romans also had a long trumpet with a hooked bell, called the *lituus*, which, apart from the shape of the bell, had a close parallel in the Celtic *carnyx*.

One of the most beautiful shapes in the world of musical instruments is surely that of the Scandinavian *lur* of the Bronze Age, with its graceful inward-turning S-shaped curves. It seems that the *lurer* were always made in pairs, and rock drawings clearly show that they were used for cult purposes. Some thirty specimens have been recovered in excellent preservation from the moors and bogs of Denmark.

(above) A Viking *lur* and *(below)* an oliphant

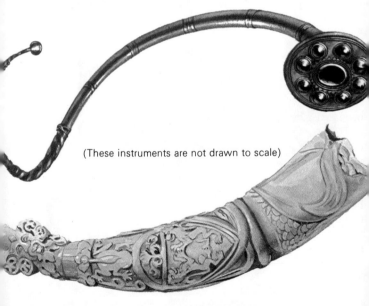

(These instruments are not drawn to scale)

Medieval straight trumpets, from an illustration in the thirteenth-century *Cantigas de Santa Maria*

The mouthpiece, which is non-detachable, is cup-shaped and their total range may have been as much as twelve harmonics. Despite their early date – probably the first half of the first millennium BC – it seems inappropriate to describe these sophisticated instruments as belonging to a primitive musical culture. Nevertheless, their shape has suggested to as eminent a musicologist as Curt Sachs, that the original *lurer* were made from mammoth tusks. If this were true, then they would confirm the general pattern of all the brass instruments originating in the use of animal horns.

The most magnificent of such animal horns to be used in the Middle Ages was the oliphant which, as its name suggests, was a section of an elephant tusk. It was often richly carved, as can be seen from the thirteenth-century example illustrated here, and is supposed to have been the type of horn that the hero Roland sounded to summon help from the armies of Charlemagne at the fateful pass of Roncevaux. According to the eleventh-century legend that recounted the deeds of Roland, his army in its dire need also sounded its horns and

45

(left) A pipe and tabor player and *(right)*
a medieval player of the tambourine.
(opposite) The *nakers* or small medieval
kettledrums from *The Feast of Herod* by
Israel van Meckenem

buisines. The name is obviously derived from the Latin
buccina (trumpet), but the instruments themselves were
straight trumpets held before the player, made of copper or
silver and with a widely flaring bell. The illustration shows
examples from thirteenth-century Spain.

As the Middle Ages progressed, the percussion section
available to the European musician gradually extended. From
the earliest surviving manuscript illustrations we have
representations of bells and bell chimes, struck with metal
hammers and usually having about eight bells to the chime.
It is not clear how these early *carillons* were used in performance, though it seems probable that they must often have
provided a programmatic element to the music. From an early
date also, it appears that small and probably tuned cymbals
were used to accompany the music of the *jongleurs*, and were
sometimes played in conjunction with shawms and double
reed pipes. The cymbals, like the shawms themselves,
were probably ultimately of Arabic origin and it was from

this source that Europe received a number of its percussion instruments, including the tambourine, other types of frame drum, and above all, the *nakers* or small kettledrums. Christians first heard the wild and terrifying beat of these high and low pitched drums in the battles of the Crusades against the armies of Islam. The *nakers* (the name is a direct transliteration of the Arabic *naqqār*) were two small drums, one slightly larger than the other, played with small paddle-shaped hammers. The body of the drum is a small copper bowl over which a vellum head is stretched by means of thongs fastened beneath the body; by tightening these thongs the head can be tuned.

And finally we come to the pipe and tabor combination. It consists of a small three-holed pipe played with the left hand, while the right strikes out the rhythm on a small two-headed drum, or *tabor*, slung from the waist or round the neck. This combination, which remained in use as an accompaniment to dances for all ranks of society throughout the Middle Ages, first appeared in southern France and northern Spain in the twelfth century, where it is still to be heard as a folk instrument.

The medieval organ

As early as the eighth century, Western Europe had imported the organ back from the Byzantine Empire where it had continued in use since Classical times. But the great organs of the early Middle Ages were less sophisticated instruments than their classical prototype, the *hydraulos*, having neither a balanced keyboard nor a mechanism of stops for selecting different ranks of pipes. This meant the heavy action referred to earlier. Furthermore, these huge machines were fitted with a number of pipes to each note, so that when a key was depressed, in addition to the bass note, there sounded a number of the harmonics above it, including perhaps the octave and the fourth and fifth above that. This corresponded to the developing practice of singing the plainsong in parallel fourths and fifths, known as *organum*, and the similiarity of the names for the instrument and the style of singing can hardly be coincidental. The failure to develop a system of stops for selecting from the numerous ranks of pipes available led to organs being built with more than one keyboard. Indeed, by the late fourteenth century a German instrument is

(left) A charming domestic scene from the fifteenth century — husband and wife together play the 'positive' organ

(right) A 'portative' organ from a painting by Hans Memlinc

recorded with three manual keyboards and one pedalboard for the feet. In the interim, various improvements to the design of the keyboard had made for a lighter action, and finally in the fifteenth century, with the development of a stop mechanism, the organ in the West had achieved all the basic features familiar in the modern instrument. But besides such huge instruments for the music of the great churches, the principle of a number of pipes blown by bellows, and under the control of a single performer, was applied to produce delightful little instruments for performing intimate chamber music, and slightly larger models suitable for accompanying a small body of singers, or for performing with other soft-toned instruments.

The first of these was the 'portative' organ, that is, one small enough to be carried from a sling over the player's shoulders. It had a single rank of pipes with a range of about one and a half octaves and was commonly used both as a solo instrument, and also to accompany the voice of the performer, or as a member of an ensemble. The wind was supplied by some form of gravity bellows worked by the left hand,

49

while the right picked out the melody on the keyboard. The second of these small organs was called the 'positive' from the Latin *positum* (placed), being too large to be carried, though it might on high ceremonial occasions join a procession of instrumentalists, the player and organ being drawn along on a low cart. With more pipes and a larger range than the 'portative', it was also blown by a second person though, as like as not, the bellows were still of the gravity type as shown in the illustration.

Conclusion

By the end of the Middle Ages instruments, formerly confined largely to dance music, the accompaniment of the *jongleurs* or the elegant love songs of the Minnesingers, and on rare occasions to amplify the musical resources of the Church, were becoming increasingly common. The range was certainly sufficiently varied : from the soft-toned portative organ to the harsh and strident sounds of the shawm; from the nasal quality of the *rebec* to the plangent tones of the harp. Numerous illustrations show groups of instruments together; bell chimes with psalteries and harps; wind instruments with *rebecs* and fiddles, and bagpipes being played with shawms. Apart from these pictorial records (sometimes unreliable sources since they may be illustrating passages from the Bible describing Hebrew rather than European musical practice), the modern editor and director of old music must rely on a few precious medieval literary sources, to a large extent, for his knowledge of the capabilities of the instruments and of the kind of music played in Court and Church in order to arrive at valid combinations for performances today. There is, however, one principle he can with confidence hold to: medieval music was as rich in mood and as vigorous in performance as anything to be heard on the classical concert platform. Sound scholarship is essential to embark on a performance of this early music, but verve, professional expertise in the techniques of its instruments and, above all, deeply felt musicianship are the indispensable needs for the making of music, from this period as from any other.

From a medieval illumination depicting the famous Minnesinger, Frauenlob, surrounded by admirers

MUSICAL INSTRUMENTS OF THE RENAISSANCE

By the sixteenth century instruments had found a firmly established place in all types of music and an increasingly large body of music was to be written expressly for them as the age of the Renaissance proceeded. However, composers were not to master fully independent instrumental styles until the seventeenth century. Much late medieval and Renaissance instrumental music was, in fact, adapted from pieces first conceived for voices. But over the centuries the professional instrumentalists had evolved conventions of technique and ornamentation, differing from instrument to instrument. These they applied as a matter of course in their performance, not only of their own dance repertoire, but also in that of the vocal music – madrigals, motets, and so forth – which composers were now describing as 'apt for voices and instruments'. When, in the fifteenth century notation of keyboard and lute music began to be used more generally, the divide between the traditions is emphasized by the fact that instead of the old vocal notation, performer-composers made use of various styles of 'tablature', a means by which letters or symbols indicated the placing of the fingers on the instrument, rather than the pitch of the notes. Until recently it has been assumed that the written music of the early periods represents the only important line of development, but careful study of Renaissance manuscripts, coupled with practical under-standing of the techniques of the instruments of the time, has shown that the practice of performers and the written notation of the composers were two interdependent elements, brought together in performance.

The lute

Of all the Renaissance instruments, one of the most important at the time and the most familiar to modern eyes, is the lute with its elegant and beautiful shape. No other instrument has been so lovingly portrayed by artists or more splendidly employed by musicians. Introduced into Europe from the lands of Islam in the late thirteenth century (the Arabic name was *al-'ud*), the instrument remained virtually unchanged in

Italian sixteenth-century lute

Lute-playing angel from a painting by Carpaccio

appearance throughout the four hundred years or more of its active life in Western music. The Persian lute had a semi-crescent shaped pegbox, whereas that of the European model was straight and turned back at an angle of ninety degrees from the neck. The body of the European lute, while retaining the characteristic half-pear shape, tended to be somewhat less deep than that of the Arabic instrument. Much more important changes, though less immediately obvious, were the addition of frets to the European lute, and the discarding of the plectrum in favour of a finger technique in the early fifteenth century. In its classic form the lute had six courses of strings, that is, it had a pair of strings to each note, tuned either in unison or at the octave. The lower strings were of gut bound with wire, the upper strings of plain gut. The frets were pieces of gut secured across the fingerboard beneath the strings, and so placed that stopping a string against each in turn, produced a series of semi-tone intervals which lent brilliance to the tone. The use of the fingers – instead of the plectrum – for plucking the strings made possible the performance of increasingly complex polyphonic works. The history of the lute in the sixteenth and seventeenth centuries was studded with a succession of brilliant virtuosi, of whom the Englishman, John Dowland, performer and composer of songs for voice and lute, was among the greatest.

Woman tuning a bass lute from a painting by Laurent de La Hire

The art of the lute builder also reached an almost unbelievable level of perfection. The finest instruments were very fragile. The body was made of ten or more narrow curved ribs anchored to a block that also carried the broad neck. The strings were attached to a tension bridge glued to the lower part of the belly. This belly or upper table greatly affected the tone of the instrument and had also to be strong enough to withstand the tension of the strings, and light enough to provide a responsive soundboard. Necessarily it was slightly thicker and was strengthened by six or eight transverse bars; nevertheless, on a fine lute, none of the wood used in the body would be more than one twelfth of an inch thick.

Unlike many instruments, the lute was rarely subjected to decorations and modifications of its shape – designed to appeal to the eye rather than the ear. Like all the great instruments of music, its design was so perfectly suited to its acoustic function, that any modification necessarily

Elaborately decorated soprano lute and detail of a decorative rose of a lute

detracted from it. Only in the fret-work 'rose', that covered the soundhole in the belly, did makers sometimes indulge in the luxury of decoration and, in the best examples, the delicate filigree work served as a foil to the simple perfection of form that surrounded it.

Such then was the lute in its classical purity. The prestige of the greatest lutanists is well illustrated by the fact that Dowland, while in the service of the Royal Court of Denmark, received a salary equal to that of the Admiral of the Fleet. The instrument enjoyed an extended vogue in France during the first decades of the seventeenth century, and continued in use – though with slowly decreasing popularity – throughout the century in all the countries of Europe. It retained a position of importance longest in Germany, where the last great virtuoso of the instrument died in the 1740s.

Other stringed instruments of the Renaissance

From the middle of the sixteenth century, as the place of instruments became more prominent and as the nature of music itself moved towards a more harmonic pattern, new instruments were developed to thicken the bass line of the music, and to strengthen the chordal structure. The basic feature of the 'archlute', as it was called, was an extension added to the neck of the normal lute to enable it to carry longer bass strings. The two main types of archlute were the *theorbo* (probably invented in Vencie in the 1750s) and the *chitarrone* which developed, possibly first at Padua, somewhat later.

The *theorbo*, designed to give greater body to the bass and harmonies of the music, had a heavier tone than the lute. This resulted from the neck being somewhat longer, so that the instrument had a greater string length. Instead of the angled pegbox of the lute, it had a straight pegbox in line with the neck that held the strings running over the fingerboard. A second pegbox, joined to the first by a short S-shaped wooden bracket which carried it out of the line of the fingerboard, was used for three or four additional 'off-board' strings that

(top) Detail of the neck of a *theorbo*, *(left)* a theorboed lute and *(right)* a *chitarrone*

A *penorcorn* which has nine pairs of strings

were not stopped but could be tuned to the bass notes of the harmony, thus further reinforcing it. Because of the longer strings, and the consequent larger gaps between the frets on the fingerboard, the *theorbo*, which was usually single strung, was less agile than the lute.

The *chitarrone* was simply a *theorbo* of inordinately exaggerated dimensions. The second pegbox was carried far beyond the first, so that the overall length of the instrument might be as great as six and a half feet, and the number of off-board strings might be as many as eight.

All the instruments so far discussed have gut strings and are strung under comparatively light tension. However, a number of other plucked instruments, flat-backed and heavily strung with wire strings, were commonly used in the sixteenth century. Most common of them all was the cittern. Smaller than the lute, and with metal, not gut frets, it had two main styles – the English and the Italian. The body of the English instrument tended to be nearly circular in shape, with the same depth at all points, while that of the Italian cittern tended to be elongated, with the back sloping inwards to the belly from neck to base. Bass citterns were known, and the seventeenth-century German theorist, Praetorius, uses the name *penorcon* for an instrument of the type. Another instrument derived from the cittern, and one that enjoyed a considerable vogue for about half a century, was the *pandora* or *bandora*, invented in the 1560s by the English maker, John Rose of London. It had six pairs of strings and a slanting nut and slanting frets that gave the bass strings a greater speaking length. Its most distinctive feature was the three lobes of the body, and these characterize the smaller version of the instrument called the *orpharion*, which had the same tuning as the lute.

(above) An English cittern and *(below)* an Italian cittern

Wind instruments of the Renaissance

In the Middle Ages and the Renaissance there were two main groups of wind instruments for 'high' and 'low' music. These terms refer to loud instruments which were suitable for the open air or large halls, and to quiet instruments used in chamber consorts. Among the reed instruments of the former category were the shawms, described by a contemporary as second only to the trumpet in volume – indeed they were often used with trumpets for martial music. Their loudness resulted partly from the widely flaring double reed with which they were sounded, and partly from the player allowing it to vibrate freely in the mouth rather than attempting to control it in the manner of the modern oboist. Like most of the medieval instruments, they were subjected to the Renaissance passion for homogeneous families of instruments, and to the originally high-pitched shawms were added bass members of the family called 'pommers'.

The soft-toned nasal sounding crumhorn was probably

(top) Crumhorns with the detachable reed cap clearly shown
(below) A pommer, the bass of the shawm family

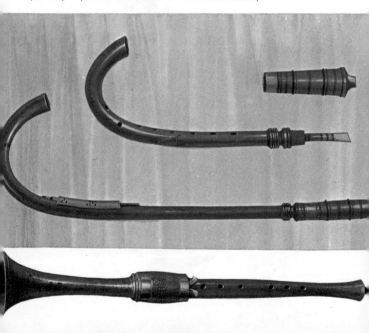

invented during the fifteenth century. It had a cylindrical bore, and a comparatively short tube turned up at the end; but, because of the acoustic properties of the cylindrical reed-blown tube, it gave far lower notes than were available, for example, on recorders of the same length. The acoustics of the tube also prevented the crumhorn from overblowing and hence it had a limited range. Its characteristic tone resulted partly from the fact that the double reed vibrated not in the mouth, but in a large cylindrical reed cap with a mouth hole at one end through which the player blew. Another instrument with a similar reed cap was the German *Rauschpfeife*, related to the shawm but with a wide conical bore. Among the innumerable invented instruments that proliferated at this time was the remarkable *racket*. With an overall length of about one foot, it could reach down about an octave below a man's bass voice. Played with a double reed, it was made of a short cylinder of wood or ivory, in which a number of parallel cylindrical channels were bored up and down, connected alternately at top and bottom to form one continuous tube.

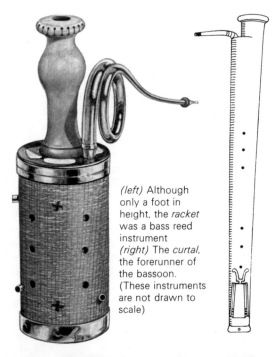

(left) Although only a foot in height, the *racket* was a bass reed instrument
(right) The *curtal*, the forerunner of the bassoon.
(These instruments are not drawn to scale)

A treble cornett dated 1605

Of more importance for the future, because it was more versatile, was the *curtal*, the ancestor of the bassoon. Also a double reed instrument, this had a conical tube (bored in only two doubled back lengths in a single piece of wood) that made available an extended range of overblown harmonics.

Besides these reed instruments an early unkeyed transverse flute was also known, but more important during the sixteenth century was the recorder. Here the air is set in vibration by a lip cut in the wall of the instrument below the mouthpiece. The breath of the player is directed on to this lip through a narrow duct between the upper wall of the tube and a wooden block called the 'fipple'. The Renaissance recorder had a wider bore than that common since the eighteenth century, and a more brilliant tone. A full family, from the high-pitched sopranino to a bass sounding the C below middle C, was developed and was very popular.

As we have seen, the fifteenth and sixteenth centuries were periods of great inventiveness in the field of musical instruments, and of all these experiments probably the most important was the trombone. The old English word 'sackbut' is often used to describe the early trombone, which had a narrower bore and less flaring bell than the modern type and hence a thinner and less blaring tone. But apart from these slight differences, the instrument has remained unchanged since its invention in the fifteenth century. For the purpose of dance music, musicians played not the long straight war trumpet, but a modification of it called the slide trumpet. The straight tube had been doubled into a flat curve and the mouthpiece was attached to a separate mouth pipe about a foot long, over which the main tube could move. By holding the mouthpiece and pipe to the lips with one hand, and shifting the rest of the instrument with the other, it was possible for the player to vary the length of the sounding tube, and thus the pitch notes. Even this limited amount of movement gave the trumpeter two or three different harmonic series to select from, and filled many of the gaps which had limited the scope of the straight trumpet. By introducing the slide into the lower 'U' bend of the slide trumpet and thus enabling the player to extend the tube without the need of shifting the greater part of the instrument, the trombone was born, Furthermore the new instrument had a complete chromatic range and was the most perfect instrument acoustically ever invented.

These strange instruments, in so far as they were sounded with a cup mouthpiece like the trumpet, had affinities with the family of brass instruments, but there the similarity ended. The cornett, a soprano instrument, was made of wood bound in leather and had fingers like the recorders. The technique was demanding, but before the introduction of valves in the nineteenth century, it was the only satisfactory high-pitched instrument of

(left) A medieval slide trumpet.
(right) A German trombone dated 1668

A player of the bass viol, from a tutor for the instrument, and detail of a pegbox

(opposite) Two examples of the classic shape of the viol

brass type, and became the preserve of a race of expert performers who were perhaps the first true virtuosi in European 'art' music. Certainly their salaries bespeak the respect in which they were held. The great Monteverdi once complained that his own income as Director of Music at the Court of Mantua was scarcely better than that of his leading cornettist.

Bowed instruments of the Renaissance
The viols
During the sixteenth century the natural evolution of the medieval fiddles and *rebecs* led to the development of the violin. Like its predecessors, this remained for the greater part of the century the instrument of popular or light dance

music. It was the viol that was cultivated by serious musicians; though it was to be ousted by the violin during the seventeenth century. The tone of the two instruments is quite distinctive, the viol's being reedier than the violin's; their construction is also different in some important respects. The viol is easily identifiable by its sloping shoulders; it also has a flat back, 'flame'-shaped holes in the belly and, most important of all, frets on the fingerboard.

Two modes of performing the viol were known – by plucking it or by bowing. The first of these, the *vihuela de mano,* bred the guitar; the second, the *vihuela de arco,* became popular with virtuosi outside Spain and seems first to have penetrated to northern Italy from the Spanish territories of the kingdom of Naples. At the beginning of the sixteenth century we find illustrations of viols that have retained several *vihuela*-like characteristics. Some have a central rose, as opposed to the side flame holes either side of the bridge; others have something of the hourglass shape of the *vihuela,* and most are shown in the early part of the century being played very awkwardly – held across the body like a modern guitar, and bowed from below.

In its technique the viol was closely allied to the bowed *vihuela,* insofar as it adapted frets and was bowed with palm upwards, but in crucial matters of construction it clearly exhibits the same ancestry as the violin. Like the violin, the viol had a high pressure bridge and tailpiece, to which

were attached the strings, as distinct from the tension bridge of the guitar. It had a convex belly and a sound-post inside the sound-box, which supported part of pressure of the bridge directly above it and amplified the vibrations within the resonating chamber. It seems likely that the viol was structurally another line of development from the medieval *rebecs* and fiddles representing a hybridization of a technique adopted from one instrument to members of another family. This appears a simpler and more rational procedure than that musicians should not only adopt the technique, and perhaps the repertory of the Spanish *vihuela de arco*, but also go to the length of completely rebuilding it in the form of the modified violin, so that finally there only remained the frets and the flat back to remind us of its ancestry among the guitars.

During the sixteenth century a whole family of viols was developed from treble to bass. From the beginning the bigger sizes were played between the legs instead of across the knees, and the name *viola da gamba* was adopted for the whole family; in time even the smaller treble viols were played rested vertically on the knees instead of being slanted across the body. The instrument became widespread throughout Europe and especially popular in the North. In England it brought about a repertoire of music composed in an elaborately polyphonic style for a group or 'consort' of different sizes of viol. This manner of composition remained in vogue until the time of Purcell, and had its imitators on the Continent.

The viol also had a considerable vogue as a solo instrument, and here the lower members of the family were preferred. From the early part of the sixteenth century, a style of highly ornamented playing had been evolved on the bass viol, and this mode of playing in 'divisions' was much cultivated in England and long remained popular in the North. The last virtuoso was the German, Karl Friedrich Abel, who as late as the 1780s was giving concerts in London in collaboration with his friend Johann Christian Bach. A second style of solo viol playing was known as the 'lyra' viol; here considerable use was made of chords playing in two or three part harmony. Often the 'lyra' viol style consisted of plucking the instrument in the manner of the lute, and a special size of viol was used, built somewhat smaller than the normal-sized bass instrument.

(left) Decorative tail-piece of a bass viol. *(right)* A *viola d'amore;* note the sympathetic strings

Keyboard instruments of the Renaissance

The stringed keyboard instruments begin to acquire their classic form during the fifteenth century, but a fascinating problem is presented by the mysterious 'eschaqueil d'Angleterre', known only from written evidence, but described in documents dating from the time of Edward III, and also in France during the late fourteenth century. Various suggestions have been offered for the interpretations of the descriptions that have survived, ranging from the possibility that it had a hammer mechanism and was thus a primitive type of piano, to the suggestion that it was a combined organ and harpsichord.

We are on firmer ground with the early history of the clavichord – structurally the simplest keyboard instrument ever devised. As with the piano or the harpsichord, the strings were stretched between two bridges, but the sounding length of the string was between one of these bridges and the metal 'tangent' which actually struck the string to produce the note. Depressing the key brought the tangent – set vertically at its further end – up

(above) The parts of the jack
(below) The action of a harpsichord

sharply against the string. So long as the key was held down, the tangent remained in contact with the string. A *vibrato* effect could be attained by moving the key, and hence the tangent, fractionally from side to side, and by varying the power with which he struck the key, the player could even command a slight variation of loudness – a feature not properly incorporated in keyboard instruments until the invention of the pianoforte in the eighteenth century. Since the speaking length of the string was between the bridge and the tangent, it was possible to make one string serve two or even three tangents, designed to strike it at different points, and thus to produce separate notes. These notes could not, of course, be sounded simultaneously but, since they were at a semi-tone or, at the most, a tone apart, there was never any occasion to do so. An instrument of this type was known as a fretted clavichord.

It seems fairly certain that the clavichord originated, perhaps in the twelfth century, from the addition of a keyed mechanism to the one-stringed monochord. This was a scientific and teaching aid used to exhibit the properties of the different intervals, and described briefly in our account of the *tromba marina*. The earliest clavichords were, then, melody instruments and probably continued to be used primarily for teaching purposes, notably for teaching singers. But by the fifteenth century instruments are known with ten or more strings, and from then on the range grew; in a number of cases the volume of the instrument was increased by providing two

A sixteenth-century clavichord

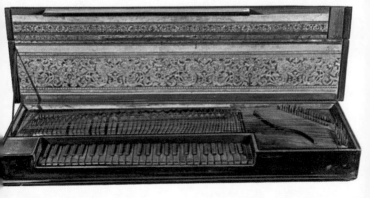

strings, tuned in unison, for one note. Throughout its career the clavichord continued to serve an important function in the practice room, being much used by organists, especially in Germany, and even being provided with two manuals and a pedalboard. Many of the preludes and fugues in the set of Forty-eight known as *The Well-Tempered Clavier* by J. S. Bach were intended for the clavichord. But the German word *Clavier* had a general significance of 'keyboard' and could be used for clavichord, harpsichord or piano.

The origins of the harpsichord, the major keyboard instrument of the sixteenth and seventeenth centuries, are possibly to be found in the addition of a keyboard action to the quills of the psaltery. However, the history of the instrument before the year 1500 is obscure.

The action of the harpsichord consists of the key and the jack. The jack is a slender pillar, rectangular in cross section, attached to the end of the key away from the player; it rises to the height of the string and passes very slightly to one side of it. When the key is at rest, a small piece of felt (projecting from the top of the jack) rests on the string and stops it reso-

A sixteenth-century Italian spinet

nating in sympathy with other strings being played. Below this is a slot, cut in the jack, in which a small wooden 'tongue' is pivoted which is held in place by a hair spring. Projecting from this is a plectrum made of quill or leather. When the key is struck, the jack moves upwards a short distance before being arrested by the key-rail that runs the length of the keyboard over the row of jacks; as it does so, the plectrum plucks the string. When the key is released the jack falls back and the damper deadens the vibrations of the string; as the quill passes the string, it is pushed back and does not pluck it a second time, being returned to its position by the light spring.

The harpsichord has a fully chromatic range of about five octaves, and the strings run down the length of the character-istically wing-shaped body of the instrument over a wooden soundboard. The jacks move up and down in a row of holes pierced near its centre-point with a decorative rose similar to

An eighteenth-century English harpsichord, showing the swell mechanism

The elaborately built seventeenth-century 'Dolphin' harpsichord

that found on the lute. The strings are stretched between sturdy pegs anchored in a wrestplank, just behind the keyboard and a curving bridge glued to the soundboard. They pass over this to be attached to a row of 'hitch pins' set in the soundboard; the strings are tuned with a T-shaped key that is used to turn the pegs in the wrestplank.

During the sixteenth century and on many standard instruments made after that, each note was provided with a single string but, as the seventeenth century progressed, each note came to be provided with additional strings controlled by a stop mechanism which allowed the player to produce different effects of pitch and tone from the instrument. Very early on, two-manual harpsichords were built, thus further extending the instrument's versatility; two contrasting tone colours being instantly available and rapid crossing passage work being made comparatively simple. Later a pedalboard was added to some instruments. During the eighteenth century, the harpsichord slowly suffered from the competition of the rapidly improving pianoforte. Graduated effects of *crescendo* and *diminuendo* were not available to the harpsichordist since, however hard he struck the key, the quill plucked the string with effectively the same force. In an attempt to meet this rivalry some harpsichords, above all in England in the second half of the eighteenth century, were fitted with a swell mechanism. This consisted of a series of close-fitting louvres forming a cover over the strings. By operating a pedal, the player could gradually open these, and thus mechanically increase the volume of sound coming from the instrument. But by this development the harpsichord had admitted its shortcomings in the world of the new sensitivity in music, and had entered the period of its decadence.

During this period also, additional effects proliferated to give increased scope for variety of tone to the instrument. But in its great classical heyday the harpsichord had been content with strings tuned to the basic pitch and – to give

An ingeniously designed
travelling harpsichord

added brilliance – strings tuned an octave above it, controlled by a stop. Some modern harpsichords are even fitted with electrical amplification systems to increase the volume. This is partly because of the larger size of the modern concert hall, but also because not all the secrets of the great makers of the past have been fully learned.

The first fine harpsichords were built in Italy, but by the second half of the sixteenth century the Flemish family-firm of the Ruckers had established a reputation that soon made them one of the most renowned firms of European instrument-makers; there were, of course, many other excellent builders of whom Jacob Kirkman, working in London in the middle of the eighteenth century, was one. The harpsichord was the primary harmonic instrument in orchestral music – the early symphonies of Haydn would have been conducted by the composer from the harpsichord on which he was playing a harmonic *continuo*. But it was also the major solo instrument of its age, and the keyboard music of composers from Byrd to Bach and Domenico Scarlatti can only be fully enjoyed on the instrument for which it was written.

Two other instruments used the action described above and differed from the harpsichord only in details of size and shape. In England, the generic term for stringed keyboard

A sixteenth-century English virginal

instruments was the virginal. The name was once colourfully thought to have derived from the fact that the instrument was played by Elizabeth I, the Virgin Queen, but unfortunately the name was known in Europe at least a century before her time. The virginal is essentially an oblong harpsichord with the strings running from left to right, that is, parallel to the keyboard rather than away from it, as in the harpsichord. This disposition of the strings is found also in the spinet, a small harpsichord with a 'leg of mutton' shape –

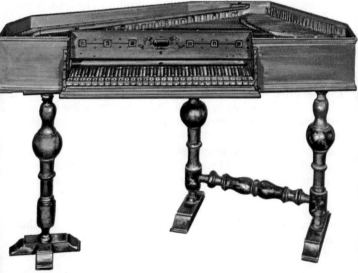

A French spinet of the seventeenth century

the longest side containing the keyboard which, in Italian spinets, projected out from the instrument. Many of the cases of all these instruments were embellished with the most lavish decoration; the inside of the lid providing the opportunity for beautiful and detailed paintings, while in the most extravagant examples, such as the 'Dolphin' harpsichord illustrated, the whole instrument was built into an elaborate sculptural allegory. Such excessive ornament was rare, of course, and throughout its long working-life the harpsichord retained its classic and elegant form.

Ceremonial music of the Renaissance

During the Renaissance the world of professional music was, as it is today, one of considerable variety. It was also a closed world and one in which professionalism was highly prized and jealously guarded. The distinction between the high and low instruments, between those used for open-air music and those for the less raucous and shrill entertainments of the salon, has been touched on. The chief instruments of this high music were the trumpets and shawms. It was these, and above all the trumpets, which provided the splendid and martial music which heralded the approach of a royal or princely procession, and gave brilliance to the high moments of municipal life.

The trumpeters were something of a race apart, and held a high opinion of themselves – and with reason. The instrument of which they were masters was a simple brass or silver cylindrical tube, some five or six feet long, folded twice to give a single flattened loop with the flaring bell pointing out from the player. Its characteristic decoration was two, often elaborately carved metal bosses (called 'garnishes') at the mid-points of the loop, and the overlapping parts of the tube were often bound together with brightly-coloured cord to give the whole instrument greater rigidity. It was on this, with only the notes of the harmonic series at their command, that the trumpeters produced the brilliant and elaborate fanfares; at the high and difficult end of the range the notes, lying closer together, could be used to play rapid melodic decorations. The control of breathing and lip, needed to ensure accurate and faultless selection of the close-lying notes, and correcting the faults of diatonic intonation inherent in the natural harmonic scale being used, were the fruit of long years of practice and considerable expertise. The guilds of trumpeters were honoured by their fellow musicians and employers and vigorously defended their privileged status. A trumpeter of sixteenth-century Nuremberg, who had the temerity to breach the guild regulations, had his playing career summarily terminated by other guild members, who broke into his house one night and smashed in his front teeth.

The players of the drums were also members of the trumpeter's guilds. They played a variety of frame drums – ancestors of the deeper tenor drum of today, and also the large

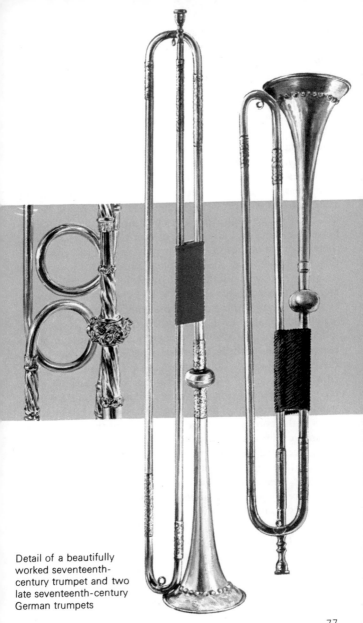

Detail of a beautifully
worked seventeenth-
century trumpet and two
late seventeenth-century
German trumpets

military kettledrums; similar to the medieval *nakers* and like those imported from the world of Islam. These large kettledrums, sometimes called *timpani*, came into Europe through its connexion with the Turkish armies during the fifteenth century. They were quickly incorporated into the tradition of ceremonial music, and the rhythms of trumpeters and drummers were among the closely guarded secrets of the 'union'.

During the seventeenth century, the woodwind underwent revolutionary improvements. The chief architects of this revolution were the members of the family of the Hotteterres, musicians and members of the royal band of Louis XIV. In France, as in many northern countries, the loud-sounding and relatively inexpressive shawms had been used in certain indoor music as well as for the open air. The young Italian-born Jean-Baptiste Lully, Louis's Master of Music, excluded them from his orchestra, and it may have been in response to this challenge that the musicians produced the *hautbois* (English, hoboy; modern oboe). By building the new instrument in three separate sections, Jean Hotteterre made possible a more accurate drilling of the bore; this, like the fingerholes, was much smaller in diameter than that of its predecessor, while the flare of the bell was much reduced. These improvements together with the use of a narrower, longer reed held in the player's mouth – and hence susceptible to much greater control – produced a reed instrument of astonishing sensitivity and delicacy. Similar kinds of changes to the old *curtal* yielded the forerunner of the modern bassoon, while modifications to the bore of the transverse flute, and the growing taste for music of nuance and subtle gradations, led to the former being accepted into the orchestra dominated by the violins, and the latter becoming a serious rival to the less expressive recorder. Nevertheless, these new wind instruments, although considered a great advance on those they displaced, still presented considerable problems of intonation in keys remote from the home key of the instrument. It was not until a further burst of inventive endeavour in the nineteenth century, that suitable key mechanisms were evolved to solve these problems.

(from left to right) A German bassoon of about 1700; an eighteenth-century oboe; an early one-keyed flute

(These instruments are not drawn to scale)

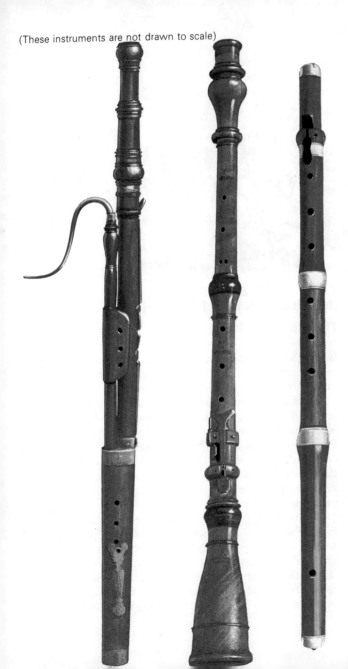

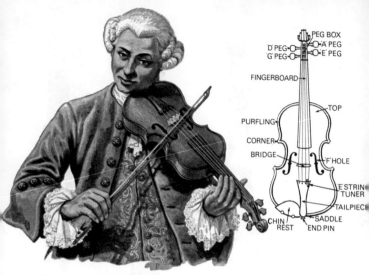

Labels on diagram: PEG BOX, D PEG, A PEG, G PEG, E PEG, FINGERBOARD, TOP, PURFLING, CORNER, BRIDGE, 'F' HOLE, 'E' STRING TUNER, TAILPIECE, CHIN REST, SADDLE, END PIN

THE DEVELOPMENT OF MUSICAL INSTRUMENTS AFTER THE RENAISSANCE

The violin family

It is the rise of the violin more than any other single factor that dominates the history of instruments during the seventeenth century. Its origins in the medieval bowed instruments, such as the fiddle, have been mentioned and its early association with dance music and the *jongleurs* led to the violin being treated during the start of its career as a somewhat secondary instrument. But in Italy, the leader of European musical taste, the violin was already being used for certain dramatic effects in the orchestras of Florence during the 1560s. Within a century its brilliant tone, great dynamic range and greater responsiveness to the demands of the performer, enabled it to triumph over the viol.

Despite its apparent simplicity of construction, the violin is made up of no fewer than seventy separate parts. The early history of the instrument is obscure, and it seems to have emerged in its essentially modern form in the middle of the sixteenth century. The first great makers were the Amati family from the north Italian town of Cremona – the home of Antonio Stradivari (1644–1737), the greatest violin-maker of

(above) The classic violin shape. *(opposite left)* This picture shows the early low grip used by violinists. *(opposite right)* Diagram of the parts of a violin

all time – and the finest Italian violins continued to be made there, and also in Brescia and Bologna. The only non-Italian masters of this period to gain an international reputation were the Austrian, Jakob Stainer (c. 1617–1683) of Absam near Innsbruck, and to a lesser degree, the Frenchman, Jean-Baptiste Vuillaume of Paris. For a long time, spanned by the careers of these men, the violin, although remaining unchanged in its general outward appearance, underwent numerous and important modifications to make it more adaptable to the needs of generations of composers and performers. Some of these we shall detail later, but first it is necessary to explain some of the main features of the design of the instrument.

The classic profile of the violin is characterized by the high shoulders of the body, the deep C-shaped centre bouts, which facilitate the passage of the bow, and the *f*-shaped soundholes on either side of the strings. The strings themselves are strung between a roughly Y-shaped 'tailpiece' and wound around lateral pegs in a pegbox finished with an elegant scroll. From the tail-piece the strings pass over a wooden openwork bridge, in the centre of the body, and an ivory nut at the top of the neck. The strings are stopped by the fingers against a finger-board glued to the top of the neck and extended down beyond it above the top or belly of the instrument. Both the top and back of the elegantly shaped body are convexly arched in order to give it greater strength to resist the tension in the strings. The side walls of the body, known as the ribs, are also reinforced with lining pieces, while the pressure of the bridge, forced down by the high tension in the strings is, in part, relieved by the soundpost placed directly under the right-hand side of the bridge and resting on the back. Finally, we should mention the bass-bar, glued against the underside of the belly and running about three-quarters of its length. Its function is not only to provide additional structural rigidity to the belly, but also to distribute the resonances of the bridges and, hence, to improve the acoustic qualities of the instrument. The finger-board and tail-piece are usually of ebony, while the various parts of the body are of different types of deciduous wood chosen for their strength and acoustic qualities. The instru-ment is finished with a fine varnish over the whole body. This is applied exclusively to protect the wood but must be care-fully prepared and applied, since unsuitable varnishing not only detracts from the appearance of the violin, but also impairs the tone. Among important modifications to the design introduced over the generations have been the extension of the fingerboard to allow for the more advanced technique of the nineteenth and twentieth centuries, and the slight lengthening of the neck, which was now thrown back at an angle. Both these changes, together with the use of a higher bridge, made possible a slightly greater string length and hence a higher tension and greater brilliance of tone.

The other members of the violin family, as it now exists, are the viola (a tenor violin in effect) and the 'cello, which both emerged only after a number of variants had been experi-mented with. Originating in a clumsy type of five-stringed bass fiddle of the mid-sixteenth century, the 'cello did not achieve a standard length for some time. Whereas the violin had had its first virtuosi in the mid-seventeenth century, it was not until the time of the Italian, Franciscello, in the first half of the next century, that a 'cellist of genius arose. Yet the sweet and less heavy tone of the bass viol continued to be

A sixteenth-century viola

preferred in northern Europe until much later.

The demands, made by nineteenth-century audiences, for still greater virtuosity in the concert hall, led to further small but important modifications in the violin and the 'cello. A chin rest was fitted to the violin allowing the performer to support the instrument entirely with a pincer-like grip of chin against collarbone. The earliest illustrations of violinists show them holding their instrument either against the chest and

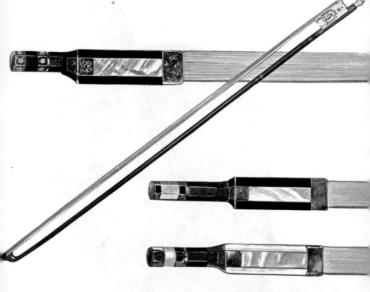

Decorative bow nuts, and an eighteenth-century convex bow

supporting it on the outstretched left arm, or loosely under the chin. Gradually the second position came to be preferred, allowing the arm and fingers of the left hand a greater degree of relaxation – and hence agility. The ultimate stage was to free the arm altogether from its supporting rôle and leave it entirely free and relaxed for the demanding fingerings that composers were now writing. A similar type of liberation for the player from secondary considerations came in the 'cello with the adoption, in the later nineteenth century, of a tailpin in a socket in the bottom of the instrument, on which the player could rest it during performances. Formerly it had been gripped between the knees, like the bass viol, rested on the floor, or on the inside of the instep of the left foot. From Italy the popularity of the violins spread to France. Already in the first decades of the seventeenth century, the French kings had had a group of twenty-four violinists, *les vingt-quatre violons du roi*, which developed into a veritable musical *élite*. The positions passed from father to son and were jealously guarded. In the orchestra of Lully the core of instrumental sound was provided by the violins, and this became the general pattern of the eighteenth-century orchestra and remained so into the nineteenth century.

However magnificent the violin, it remains silent without the bow. This too had been the subject of much refinement, until the modern bow is now something of a precision instrument, carefully balanced and fitted with an adjustable nut. This nut can vary the tension in the 'ribbon' of horsehair strung between it and the tip of the concave stick. At first

A violin in Delft faience — intended only to be looked at

the violin bow, like that of the viol, had an outward curving stick and, although the violin was bowed palm downwards, the bow was gripped some distance from the nut, with the thumb pinching the hair. Later, as the stick was straightened and then reversed in its curve, the grip was shifted down towards the nut. All these developments led to a greater flexibility in the use of the bow and different bowing techniques.

The largest member of the violin family is the double bass. Most examples have a flat back and sloping shoulders – modifications adopted to make the manipulation of so cumbersome an instrument somewhat easier – though early sixteenth-century examples have the arched back characteristic of the violin family. Another modification on the standard violin pattern is that the strings are tuned in fourths rather than fifths. Throughout the three centuries of its history the double bass has never achieved either a standard size or a standard number of strings. The usual size now in use is about 180–200 cm. (6–6½ ft.) and there are generally four strings, though three- and five-stringed basses have often been used and are still occasionally to be met with.

There have been a number of freak instruments, of which perhaps the most fascinating was the *octobasse*, built by Vuillaume in 1849, which required a mechanism of crank-operated levers to enable the player to stop the strings. Between this monster, and the beautiful examples of the instrument-maker's craft illustrated on this page, lies the huge and varied range which is to be found in the world of musical instruments. By and large miniature instruments such as these were made to suit a rich amateur's fancy, but at least one example – that of the pocket violin – was of practical value. Called a *pochette* (from the French *poche*, meaning pocket), or in English, the kit, it was ideally suited for the dancing-master, who, needing in turn to play the music for his pupils and then demonstrate the steps to them, could house it in his pocket. But the *pochette*, or *sopranino* violin, as it might also be called, was actually used in the orchestra and was asked for by Monteverdi in one of his operatic scores.

1 A walking-stick clarinet, **2** a walking-stick violin with its bow and cover and **3** a dancing-master's kit

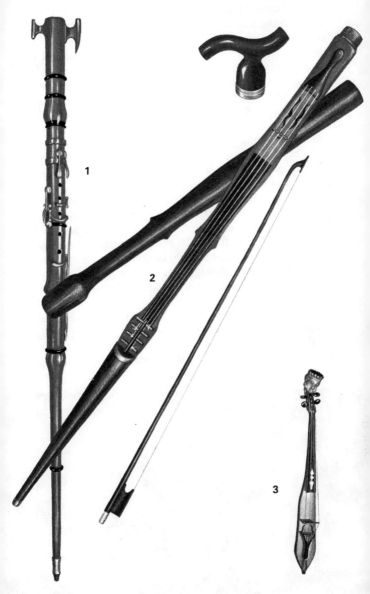

The Baroque organ

So far we have traced the development of the organ from its Roman origins to the early Renaissance. During the Age of the Baroque it reached a classic level of excellence and was the vehicle for some of the greatest music ever written. It was never again to win the same degree of prestige with composers; therefore we shall discuss not only the musical possibilities of the Baroque organ but also describe the basic features of the elaborate action of the instrument.

Until the twentieth century this action was entirely mechanical. Most modern organs make use of electric circuits and small pneumatic devices to lighten the touch of the instrument and to make for ease of playing. A growing body of players are coming to the opinion, however, that the best mechanical or 'tracker' actions of the past give the player more direct contact with the pipes, and hence greater responsiveness. Just as in other fields, the present generation is showing an ever-growing interest in early instruments. Europe is being searched for organs dating from the Renaissance and early Baroque periods which have avoided the improvements of later ages. As often as not, this has happened where the authorities lacked the money to pay for the adaption of their fine old instruments to the changing fashion. The building of organs has always been an expensive business; not only did the builders have to be paid, but also it was usually felt advisable

(left) Small
'positive' organs
were used on
processions
(above) A Bible
Regal

to call in an expert performer to give a report on the instrument before completion of the order was made. J. S. Bach, the most famous organist of his own, or indeed any other time, was often called upon to give such reports, and it was in Germany that the instrument enjoyed its highest development and prestige. We must not, of course, forget such great figures as the Itailian, Girolamo Frescobaldi, or the Frenchman, François Couperin. But it was, above all, in Protestant Germany where the instrument played a major part in the service of the Lutheran Church and the advanced contrapuntal style of composition which culminated in the work of Bach himself, was evolved.

Bach's organ at Arnstadt had three departments, controlled by two manuals and a pedalboard. During his day, three-manual instruments were fairly common and, although subsequently four manuals have become pretty standard

and some large instruments have as many as seven, most of the greatest music in the repertoire can be played on a two-manual instrument. In effect, the player controls three or more separate organs. Each key on the manual or the pedalboard gives the player control of a number of different pipes set in ranks over the wind chest. Depressing the finger-key, or the pedal, activates a system of wooden rods (the 'trackers') which opens a 'pallet' under the pipes of the required pitch. Which of these pipes is in fact sounded is controlled by the 'stops'. Operating one of these moves is a 'slider' – a wooden rail pierced at intervals with holes; when these holes are under the pipes, they are free to receive wind as the player opens the pallets by depressing the keys. Such are the bare essentials of the organ's actions. Sliders, controlled by stops at the 'console', enable the player to select the ranks of pipes that he wishes to use; pallets controlled by the keys enable him to let air into the pipes of the rank that he wishes to sound.

The Baroque organ of northern Germany was built primarily for the performance of contrapuntal music, and since in this kind of music all the different parts are of equal importance, it is essential that they are all heard with equal clarity. Consequently the characteristic tone of the organ was brilliant and was marked by the extensive use of 'reed' stops and 'mixtures'.

There are two basic types of organ pipe: the flue pipes, in which the sound is produced on the same principle as the recorder, and the reed pipes, in which it is produced by a small metal tongue, or reed, vibrating against an opening in the pipe. The former is generally smooth and well rounded in tone, made of wood or metal, and provides the basic 'diapason' tone of the organ; the latter, always made of metal, is more incisive. Innumerable variations could be made on these basic tone colours. Stopping the end of a flue pipe has the strange acoustic result of lowering the pitch of the pipe by an octave and also changes its tone; other methods adopted were altering the shape of the pipes and the dimensions of the reeds.

(left) Bach's organ at Arnstadt
(right) A magnificent Baroque organ-case

ORGANO   CHRISTO   CAN

A nineteenth-century double-bass clarinet and *(bottom)* the bassett horn, often used by Mozart

Newcomers to the orchestra

Not only the Romantic organ, but more especially the Romantic orchestra presented quite a different range of tone colours from anything that had gone before. This resulted from the introduction of instruments such as the trombone – not regularly used in the orchestra before the nineteenth century – from the changing balance in the instrumental forces, and also from the use of entirely new instruments.

One of these instruments, which became of increasing importance, was the clarinet. Although invented or perfected in the early years of the eighteenth century, the instrument was not given serious attention by composers until Mozart had shown its full capabilities both in *ensemble* and solo music. The principle of the single beating reed, familiar to the organ builders and also to folk musicians, was not used in the orchestra before the development of the clarinet by the German maker and musician, Johann Christoff Denner of Nürnberg.

He seems to have taken as his starting-point the *chalumeau* – a simple reed pipe with a cylindrical bore. The name has survived to designate the lowest of the three markedly different and contrasting registers of the clarinet. In the latter part of the eighteenth century a tenor instrument was added to the clarinet family; it was made of three angled joints terminating in a metal bell, and was known as the basset horn. It, too, was used by Mozart and is sometimes revived now for performances of his music.

An eighteenth-century ivory clarinet

Instruments outside the orchestra
The guitar and mandolin

In Spain the four-stringed guitar was the popular form of the 'aristocratic' *vihuela*. Whereas the latter had six pairs of strings, the guitar had only four. This instrument, for long known as *guitarra* or *gittern*, is found mentioned in catalogues of instruments as early as the fourteenth century. In the fifteenth century its popularity spread from Spain to Italy, via the Spanish Kingdom of Naples, and thence to France. Its popularity, especially amongst amateurs, continued strong. It features often in fashionable portraits and artistic allegories from the seventeenth and eighteenth centuries. In the late sixteenth century, one further change was made – this was the addition of the fifth string, or pair strings. The instrument in this modified form became known as the Spanish guitar and the name has remained. During the eighteenth century, as the guitar became more and more the instrument of amateurs, the stringing was simplified by having only one string to each course instead of two, as formerly. The shape of the instrument also changed to present a more markedly figure-of-eight outline, and the decorative rose that had sometimes been provided in the central soundhole of earlier guitars was dispensed with.

For much of its life the guitar was relegated to a secondary position in the world of music. During the nineteenth century, however, a small number of Spanish players increased the instrument's vogue in the rest of Europe, but it was not until the twentieth century that it once more received the attention of major composers. The revival in the instrument's fortunes was largely due to the famous Spanish virtuoso, Andres Segovia, for whom many leading contemporary composers have written; his example has been followed by non-Spanish musicians, notably Julian Bream of England and John Williams of Australia. But historically the guitar has always been popular as an accompaniment to the voice and is now the preferred instrument of 'pop' musicians.

Another plucked instrument which enjoyed a certain vogue in eighteenth-century society was the wire-stringed mandolin. In its original form it was soprano in pitch, but its twentieth-century revival has been built in larger sizes and is used as a consort instrument in the mandolin bands which are popular in certain parts of the world. It is fretted, like the guitar, has four strings, and is characterized by the deeply-vaulted form of its body.

A lady guitarist from a painting by Peter Lely and an eighteenth-century guitar – notice the lack of waist

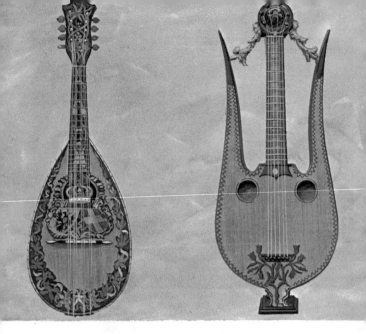

(left) A mandolin and *(right)* a nineteenth-century lyre guitar

Vogue instruments

From the seventeenth century on, when the musette bagpipe had enjoyed fashionable favour, the main stream of European music was accompanied by a secondary course of vogue instruments. By and large these had little more than a passing society appeal. But just as the art of the woodwind instrument-makers may have been refined by the demands of producing the beautiful little *musettes* – and this may in turn have led to improvements to the standard woodwind by Hotteterre and his colleagues – so some of the instruments that were the rage of society in their day, but are now obsolete, attracted the attention of major composers.

Among these was the *baryton*, a bass instrument of the viol type, that, like the *viola d'amore*, evolved during the later part of the seventeenth century. However, it was only when it was taken up by Haydn – whose patron, Prince Nicolas of Esterházy, was a devotee – that it received the concentrated attention of a major composer. Haydn wrote over 175 works for this immensely difficult instrument. Like the bass viol it had a fretted fingerboard and six bowed strings. The character and difficulties of the *baryton* were determined by the fact that in addition to these bowed strings, it had some forty sympathetic strings passing under the fingerboard, some of which could be plucked by the thumb of the left hand.

Today we can only imagine the shimmering effect produced by this cloud of sympathetic resonance, whose only parallel in contemporary musical experience is to be found in the sound of the Indian *sitār*. But such ethereal sounds were much to the taste of the later eighteenth century. The most remarkable example was the aeolian harp, which emerged in the early years of the seventeenth century and enjoyed considerable popularity among the poets and literati of the Romantic generation. In one important respect this was not a true musical instrument, for it was sounded by natural, not by human agency. Like the bamboo chimes, whose hollow tinklings in the breeze of a

A nineteenth-century Spanish guitar

summer night delighted the ears of the courtiers of Imperial China, the aeolian harp (named after Aeolus – god of the winds) was 'played' by the wind. It consisted of a wooden frame fitted with gut strings of differing thicknesses, which vibrated in chords at the breath of the wind.

But of all these vogue instruments the one that exercised the greatest fascination over the eighteenth-century ear, was the glass harmonica. The sound is generated by drawing a moistened finger round the rim of a wine glass. These 'musical glasses', filled with water to different levels to give different pitches, can still be heard; the German vituoso, Bruno Hoffmann, has devoted himself to reviving the technique and the music for the instrument – which includes in its repertoire a number of works by Mozart. The musical glasses of this type, sounded either by friction or struck with felt-covered sticks, were known in Europe certainly from the fifteenth-century, and Gluck won some fame for himself as a performer on the instrument. But the glass harmonica proper – the instrument for which Mozart in fact wrote several works – was the invention of the American scientist and statesman,

From a contemporary picture of Benjamin Franklin playing his glass harmonica

Benjamin Franklin who, in 1761, introduced a much improved model. Here, glasses of different sizes, pierced at their base and threaded on a spindle, were revolved through a trough of water by a treadle, the performer playing the instrument as though it were a keyboard. Several players gained overnight reputations on the new instrument, which must have affected eighteenth-century ears much as the strange and disembodied sound of the *ondes martenot*, (an electrophonic instrument), affect the ears of an audience in our time.

Freakish as the *baryton* and the glass harmonica seem today, it is worth noting that they were only an extreme expression of the passion for 'sensibility' which was gaining ground during the eighteenth century and, in fact, lay behind the modifications to the more conventional instruments that had been produced in the seventeenth century. We have seen the violin displace the viol, the oboe taken up in preference to the shawm and the flute instead of the recorder. The process was not always immediate, but in every case the new instrument had offered the player a more intimate and sensitive control of the sound. The violinist, free from the frets of the viol found his fingers in more direct contact with the string; the oboist, by bringing the reed under his lips, exercised greater control over the oboe than had his predecessor on the shawm.

The *baryton* and *(left)* detail of the soundboard

The rôle of the orchestra

During the Renaissance instruments had differed widely, one from another, and the endeavour had been to emphasize these different tonal colours throughout the full range of the compass. The various instruments inherited from the Middle Ages were provided with relations of the same type, to provide a single family covering the gamut. But the Renaissance musician rejoiced in strong contrasts both of loudness and softness and of tone quality; nuance was achieved not by graduated effects on a single instrument, but by the interplay of different instruments.

As the improved instruments gave performers greater scope, not only for technical virtuosity in terms of rapid passage work – virtuosity which had been bound by commonly understood and accepted conventions – but also in terms of dynamic expressiveness, it is not surprising that the rôle of the conductor gradually became more important. Legend

Orlando Lassus, the Renaissance composer, surrounded by his musicians

has it that Lully died of a festered foot after an injury he inflicted on himself with the heavy staff that he was using to thump out the time. One hopes that the story may be true, as no more fitting end can be envisaged for the devious and pushing Master of the Royal Chapel of Louis XIV. True or not, however, the tale does illustrate the comparatively primitive rôle of the conductor in earlier periods. Always needing to control and direct the self-opinionated talents of singers, he became increasingly important during the eighteenth century until, with the revolutionary improvements to orchestral techniques achieved by the Mannheim orchestra during the 1770s and 1780s, he began to emerge as the master and director of the orchestra – a position that was only emphasized and strengthened in the nineteenth century.

The piano

The piano, the best-known and most popular of all musical instruments, is an instructive example of the difficulties of classification. Its sound is produced by the vibration of strings, but the strings themselves are set in motion, not by being plucked or bowed, but by being struck with a percussive action. It is also unlike any of the instruments of the pre-electronic age in a vital respect. Of all musicians the pianist is the only one who, at the very moment when the sound is produced, has no contact whatsoever with the sound-producing agent. When the piano hammer hits the string it is in free flight, and the player's art must be applied before the string is hit, in the sensitivity with which he operates the key.

Scholars have detected hints of piano action in the 'eschaqueil d'Angleterre', and also in somewhat later descriptions of unidentified instruments, but no evidence has yet come to light that can rob the Italian, Bartolommeo Cristofori, of the prestige of being the inventor of the pianoforte. He was born in Padua in 1655, but it is fitting that his great invention should have been made at Florence – the home of so much in European culture – where he was in the service of the dukes of Tuscany from 1698. The action of a *gravicembalo col pian e forte*, which he perfected, was described in 1711 in the *Journal of Italian Letters* by the Marchese Scipione di Maffei, and was probably completed some two years earlier. Cristofori's claims are justified not only by priority, but also because he devised an action which solved all the basic problems involved and which is, in all its fundamentals, followed in the most modern instruments. For the main problems of the piano lie in the action. Since the hammer is out of the player's control at the vital moment of contact with the string, it is essential for him to make this control before that point as precise as possible. It is crucial to enable the player to launch the hammer with as much or as little power as he wishes and to protect him against the possibility of the key, once having struck the hammer, 'bouncing' back a second time to hit the string. Cristofori's so-called 'double action' met all these difficulties and his instruments were not to be bettered in essentials for a century. For the main drawback of his pianos was one which he did not have the technology to solve: the

(above) The trade label of Clementi
(below) An eighteenth-century upright piano

hammer, thanks to his action, could be delivered against the string with greater force than the string itself – at the comparatively low levels of tension possible on a wooden frame – was able to exploit. Only with the perfection of the iron frame by the American, Alpheus Babcock of Boston, in the 1820s, could really high tension string be allowed for.

The essence of the double action was the escapement. This enabled the blow to impart its full force to the hammer without fouling it on its fall back to the rest position. In the Cristofori action (which was taken up by the German maker, Gottfried Silbermann, and through his pupil, Johann Zumpfe, transmitted to the English school) the escapement was on the key itself and the hammer was pivoted on the frame. It was this arrangement, with various refinements, which proved the best solution to the problems involved, and since it came back to the main stream of piano-building via the English school, it came to be known as the English action. However, the first major composer to explore the full possibility of the piano was Mozart, and the instrument that he used, made by Johann Andreas Stein of Vienna, employed a different system, which reached perfection in the late eighteenth century. In this Viennese action the escapement formed part of the frame, while the hammer was attached to the key. The drawback of the Stein piano was that repeated notes were difficult on it. But since the string tension, the frame and the weight of the hammer were carefully balanced, the tone was true and the dynamic range considerable.

As has been mentioned earlier, the main improvements concerned the frame. Both the demands of the composers and the muscularity of the new styles of playing obliged the makers to provide sturdier instruments, with heavier and more resilient actions. As the nineteenth century progressed, the piano, responding to the new demands put on it by the works of Beethoven, Chopin and finally Liszt, developed into an instrument of unheard-of power and responsiveness, capable of rendering both the crashing *fortes* of a Liszt piano concerto and the singing *cantabile* of a Chopin nocturne.

The makers who contributed to this progressive refinement and extension were numerous. Among the most important were Broadwood in England, Érard in France, and Steinway in

(right) The 'pyramid' piano — another eighteenth-century form of upright
(below) The nineteenth-century 'giraffe' piano

Germany, who produced the most successful of the iron frames, and in this respect provided a prototype for future builders. The most important of the early improvements were the Érard double action which appeared in the 1820s. Refining the 'English' action, so that the hammer did not fall back fully while the key was still depressed, made possible very rapid repeated notes. Other improvements were the introduction of felt hammers in place of the buckskin-covered ones of earlier models, and the perfection of the damper system, so that the vibrations of the strings are quickly and effectively deadened when the key is released. When the player wishes to sustain a note, or chord, he can raise all the dampers together by operating a foot pedal; another pedal enables him to reduce the volume of the instrument, and also its tone, by shifting the keyboard a small distance to one side, so that the hammers strike only one, or two, of the three strings of a note.

From a very early period piano makers had been producing small pianos primarily for domestic use. Among the first of these was the square piano, introduced in the mid-eighteenth century and enjoying a long and marked popularity in England. It was oblong in shape like a virginal, and the strings ran the length of the instrument, parallel with the keyboard. In the eighteenth century too, the upright piano was invented. At first, it was simply a grand piano of which the tail, instead of projecting horizontally, was turned through a right angle, so that the piano could be placed close up against the wall of the room. Some of the early uprights took on bizarre shapes – the 'giraffe' piano being a good example. However, from 1800 more and more makers adopted the important improvement of running the strings of the upright down to the floor and thus saving considerably on the height of the instrument. It was upright pianos of this type that became a standard feature of the Victorian drawing-room. German makers also established an extensive export trade of uprights to Australia, where the obsession of the colonial society with all aspects of Victorian respectability made the piano indispensable.

The mechanism of a modern upright and *(below)* of a grand piano

THE AGE OF IMPROVEMENTS

The woodwind instruments

During the nineteenth-century the design of the woodwind, so importantly improved during the seventeenth, took another step forward and the result was the instruments which we see in the woodwind section of the orchestra today.

There were three main problems. The first concerned the tonal colour, which was not homogeneous throughout the whole compass. In the case of the clarinet the difference in tone between the low, middle and high registers was so marked, that it became a feature of the instrument that is still admired. But the oboe suffered from small variations of tone, except in the hands of the most skilled players. A still more troubling inconsistency was that of intonation; various notes in the compass could not always be relied upon when some instruments, notably the flutes, were played too loudly. Finally, this problem of intonation presented another aspect when the music was in a key remote from the natural key of the instrument. In this case so many of the notes could be achieved only with difficult cross-fingering, involving awkward shifts of finger position, that only the finest virtuosi ventured to play in those keys and, naturally, preferred to have a musically sophisticated audience that had some appreciation of the problems involved. Pieces which today serve as elementary exercises for the student were once too demanding for any but the finest performers.

The eighteenth-century instruments were in many cases quite adequate for the music that they were called upon to play, and their complex and highly characteristic sounds can still be appreciated today. But, as composers came to write through the keys with increasing freedom, the need for further improvements was recognized on all hands, despite the conservative opposition of the players themselves to mechanization. By the early 1800s even this was weakening,

(above) An early bass flute, *(left) The Fifer Boy* from a painting by Edouard Manet and *(right)* a modern orchestral flute

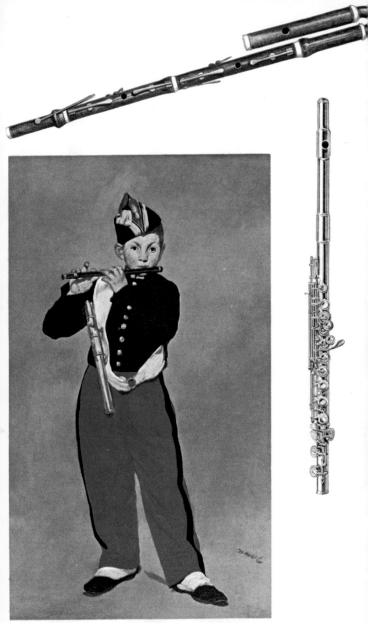

and the stage was set for the acceptance of any improvements.

The root of the instrument-maker's problem was one of materials and the engineering of the job. Keys were known of course – before the end of the eighteenth century a seven-keyed flute was gaining acceptance. Makers were also aware of the need for the correct placing of the holes and vital advances in often seemingly small details of construction made possible what amounted to a revolution in instrument-making during the nineteenth century.

The flute

The greatest successes of the innovators were achieved on the flute, where the improvements were due primarily to the work of one man, Theobald Boehm, an inventor in other fields, and a lover of the flute. Boehm devoted himself not only to improving the mechanism – and hence simplifying the fingering – but also to improving the tone. He made a thorough and preparatory study of the instrument's acoustics and then set about designing a flute with the widest possible fingerholes to give the flute greater power. Later, still pursuing his acoustic concerns, Boehm changed the inverted-conical bore of the flute to a cylindrical one, since the greater volume of air would produce a fuller and clearer tone, and redesigned the head, giving it a parabolic curve. The mechanics of Boehm's keys had two important features: the keys were mounted on axels running the length of the instrument and they were made more accessible to the fingers of the player by the use of ring keys. These were simply rings of metal round an open hole and connected by axel rods to the rest of the system, which enabled the player to close not only the hole beneath his finger, but also another one some distance from it.

Boehm introduced his flute in 1832, and though it suffered some opposition because of its heavier tone quality, it was generally adopted. Boehm, and other makers, soon devised new systems of keys for other members of the woodwind

---

(from left to right) A *heckelphone;* an eighteenth-century oboe; a *cor anglais;* a modern orchestral oboe
These instruments are not drawn to scale.

family, and also improved other aspects of the design. Softer padding for the keys, which made for a more air-tight seal, was first used on the clarinet. Later, the holes of the instrument were provided with slightly raised rims, so that the seal of key-pad to instrument was even tighter. However, on the oboe, and especially the bassoon, the design modifications intended to make the intonation of the old instruments more reliable and homogeneous, had serious effects on the tone quality, which demanded the utmost ingenuity of the inventors to overcome. The instrument in most common use in America and northern Europe

A nineteenth-century bassoonist from a painting by Degas

was evolved by the Heckel family in Germany.

New instruments

The great extension of the resources of the orchestra by the nineteenth-century composers was paralleled and complemented by the introduction of new instruments. From the time of Beethoven the trombones became full members, but that great orchestral innovator, Hector Berlioz, also made frequent use of the *piccolo*, a small high-pitched instrument of flute type, and the *cor anglais* – the alto member of the oboe family whose strange name has never been satisfactorily accounted for. Wagner's interest in a wide-bore baritone instrument of the oboe family probably gave rise to the enthusiasm which prompted the Heckel family to produce the *heckelphone*. This instrument was entirely in keeping with the desire of contemporary composers to fill out the orchestra, so that all its characteristic tones could be heard at all pitches. It was this same desire to extend the range of the orchestra that led to the

(left) A French bassoon dated 1862 and *(right)* a modern German bassoon

(from left to right) A soprano saxophone; an early nineteenth-century clarinet; a modern orchestral clarinet; a bass clarinet

introduction of bass members of the clarinet family and the construction of the double bassoon which, despite its monstrous proportions, is still seen in the orchestra today. The contrabass clarinet is also slowly gaining in popularity outside the concert hall.

Modern woodwind instruments and their players are uniquely concerned with mechanism and every maker of repute has his own refinements to offer. But there are broad national differences in design and style of performance. The most generally accepted in the field of design are the French School oboe, the Boehm flute and the French Triébert clarinet. In the case of the bassoon, however, the French model designed by Buffet of Paris is now entirely displaced in England by the German Heckel bassoon. Although its fingering is more difficult, the latter 'speaks' much more reliably and is less buzzing in tone. The difference between the two instruments and the two styles is great enough almost to suggest instruments of different families. Similar though lesser distinctions are to be found between the woodwind instruments and players of all the main national schools, so that the international woodwind virtuoso is something of a rarity.

Benny Goodman, one of the greatest virtuosi on the clarinet

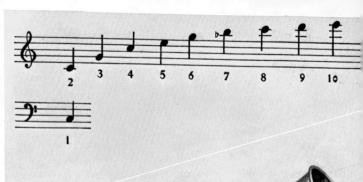

The brass instruments
The horn

The history of the modern orchestral horn begins in the sixteenth century, probably when Courts in Central Europe adopted a form of wide-bore, tightly coiled, metal instruments in favour of the animal horns which had commonly been used in the hunting field until then. It is possible that these instruments, although somewhat limited in range, may have found some use in other types of music, though always in consorts of their own kind. The next important step seems to have taken place in France, about a century later, with the development of a horn of much narrower bore and of only a single large loop. It was from this that the modern horn was to develop, and it is interesting to note that in English-speaking countries the orchestral horn is still sometimes loosely referred to as the 'French' horn. In France it was restricted to the hunting field until the 1730s, though elsewhere it had by now come into fairly common use for open-air public entertainments, and in Germany and England it had been introduced into the orchestra.

The 'natural' horn consisted of a metal tube in the form of a drawn-out cone, about twelve feet long (360 centimetres), wound in two circles about eighteen inches (45 centimetres) in diameter, and terminating in a widely flaring bell. The instrument just described was said to be pitched in F, since the lowest note available was the F below the bass clef; above this, the hornist could play only the notes of the harmonic series which offered only a continuous scale, from about middle C on the piano, upwards. The length of the horn determined its pitch, and at first, to play in different keys, the horn player had to use different horns. From the 1720s onwards this could be avoided when hornists began to use additional coils of tubing called 'crooks', which were inserted between the end of the instrument and the mouthpiece. In this way the performer was saved the inconvenience and expense of a set of different horns, and could change the pitch of his instrument – given a few bars rest in the music – with

Early attempt at fitting valves to the horn and diagram showing the intervals of the harmonic series

comparative ease. However, although he could vary the pitch, he still only had the notes of the harmonic series at his disposal.

An important improvement in the situation was made, again in about the 1720s, by a hornist in the Dresden Court orchestra – Anton Joseph Hampel. The horn had originally been held with the bell facing upwards, away from the player, as it had been in the hunting field. Some orchestral players began to hold it in the downward position, with the bell pointing away from the audience. Hampel, attempting to soften the strident tone of the instrument still further, and perhaps inspired by the example of the oboists who dampened the volume of their instruments by introducing cotton or felt pads into the bells, found that the horn could be muted by thrusting the hand into the bell. More important, he discovered that if the hand was forced right into the bell the pitch of certain notes of the instrument was raised by the interval of a semi-tone. Although the quality of these 'hand' notes was never completely satisfactory – they were always somewhat muffled in timbre – nevertheless the new notes filled some all-important gaps in the range, so that as virtuosi began to master the new technique, composers had at their disposal an instrument with exciting possibilities in solo work. It was for this hand horn that Beethoven wrote his horn sonata, and Mozart several brilliant concertos and a horn quintet.

But the hand notes could only be produced in the upper half of the range and attempts were made to extend the chromatic scale of the instrument lower, and also to correct the imperfections of tone quality. In any case, satisfactory work in the upper registers required specialization, and hornists – as the trumpeters before them – became divided into two groups: those capable of high-lying parts and those who limited themselves to the less demanding passages.

The aim of all the aforesaid experiments was to find a method of changing the pitch of the whole instrument simultaneously. Some remarkable machines were produced, the one, illustrated here, consisting of seven instruments blown from the same mouthpiece. However, the main line of

An early nineteenth-century valve mechanism. *(right)* This curiosity was effectively seven instruments in one

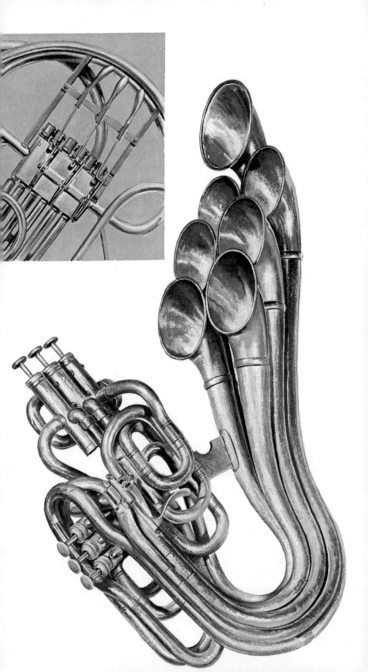

development lay in a system of valves which were operated by the movement of pierced pistons, or by rotary devices that diverted the air stream through different passages. These valves either cut out certain lengths of tube ('ascending' valves, since they raised the pitch of the instrument) or opened certain lengths of tube ('descending' valves).

The real breakthrough was made, again in Germany, by patented mechanisms brought out in the 1810s. Improvements continued throughout the nineteenth century and into the present one. Although the range was now chromatic in some models, the upper notes were liable to 'crack', even with expert players. The horn most generally in use today is the wide-bore 'German' horn with rotary descending valves, whose notes speak more easily and are more reliable than those of the narrow-bore French horn with ascending valves, though at the expense of a certain 'tubbiness' of tone. The hand in the bell has continued to be used both for fine tuning adjustments and also for certain muting effects.

Valved brass and tubas

The application of valves to the trumpet is described later – there was even a certain vogue for a valved trombone. More important, however, was the scope that the valve mechanisms offered for the building of a whole new range of bass brass instruments. From the 1830s, a miscellaneous assortment of bass valved bugles began to appear for use by military bands and in open-air music. They belonged to the bugle family, in the sense that they were wide-bore instruments with a conical tube – like the horn – but played with a cup-shaped mouthpiece – like the trumpet. By the middle of the century these instruments, particularly in the hands of French makers, were gaining in popularity and it is at this point that the talented Belgian, Adolphe Sax, entered the field. He improved the valves in certain details, and also built a complete family of valved bugles, from double bass to soprano, which he called 'saxhorns' and attempted to patent. From Sax's work, and the various other instruments produced at this time, derive the euphoniums, *flugelhorns* and tubas of the modern brass band – so popular in England – and the orchestral tuba.

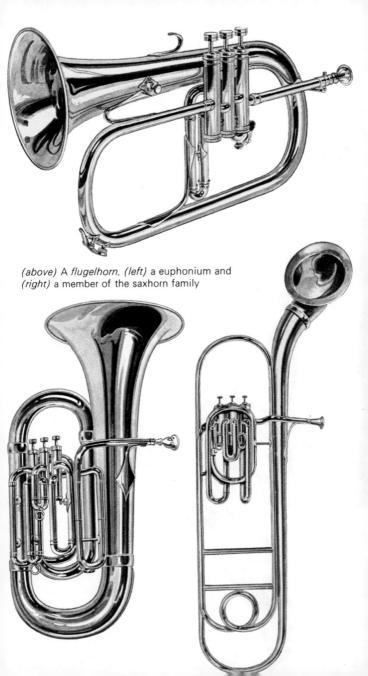

(above) A *flugelhorn, (left)* a euphonium and *(right)* a member of the saxhorn family

Keyed brass instruments

Valves, although the most effective, were not the first attempt to provide horns and trumpets with a complete chromatic range. We have already studied the Renaissance cornett, with its conical bore, cup mouthpiece and fingerholes. In the last years of the sixteenth century a bass member of the family was invented; this was the serpent, deriving its name from its curvilinear shape, and made up of wooden sections, bound together with leather. It had six large fingerholes which, in due course, were fitted with keys. It was first used in France and seems to have been intended to strengthen the plainsong line in Church worship, but from the mid-eighteenth century, first in Germany and then in England, it came into the military band. Despite its awkward and unre-

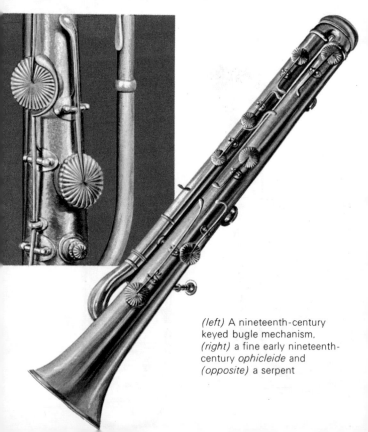

(left) A nineteenth-century keyed bugle mechanism, *(right)* a fine early nineteenth-century *ophicleide* and *(opposite)* a serpent

liable qualities, the serpent too had its virtuosi. One, a German bandsman, could apparently play flute concertos on this unwieldy instrument! In the late eighteenth century varieties of the serpent appeared, made of wood or metal and with two straight tubes linked by an elbow joint; one such variant was the confusingly named 'Russian bassoon'.

Also at this time, some European makers were experimenting with key mechanisms fitted to the trumpet – it was for a keyed trumpet that Haydn wrote his trumpet concerto – and the bugle. The most important and successful of these keyed bugles was the brass *ophicleide* introduced by a Frenchman, Jean-Hilaire Asté of Paris, in 1817 but not granted a patent until March 24, 1921, long after it had been displaced by the valved tubas. Nevertheless, the *ophicleide* had a distinctive tone – Mendelssohn scored for it in his *Midsummer Night's Dream* – and continued in use in French and Italian military bands into the early years of the twentieth century. It also had a fairly long life as an orchestral instrument, providing a bass for the trombones and occasionally being given a solo billing – the first Promenade Concert audiences in London were sometimes regaled with an *ophicleide* solo. The instrument consisted of a single U-shaped conical tube, and was played with a cup mouthpiece and fitted with between nine and twelve keys. Originally described as '*ophicleide*, or a serpent with keys', it was a much more successful instrument than its forerunner, which never won a place in serious orchestral music.

Trumpets and trombones

From the time of Bach and Handel the trumpeters, whose high professional standing outside the concert hall has been described, had also been some of the most admired virtuosi of the orchestra. Their instrument, like the horn, was limited to the notes of the harmonic series; but the tradition of florid trumpet fanfares stretched back to the Middle Ages and had bred a race of performers whose astonishing skill is revealed for us by the parts – such as the famous trumpet *obbligato* of Bach's second *Brandenburg Concerto* – that were written for them. Such high-lying and demanding passages were the preserve of a coterie of specialists known as *clarino* players, who devoted their careers to perfecting the exacting technicalities of lip and breathing that alone made such parts playable.

The instrument used by the *clarino* players was quite different from the modern trumpet. Not only did it not have valves, it was also much longer – about seven feet (2 metres) – and consequently lower pitched and had a softer, more flute-like tone, which blended far more aptly with strings and woodwind than the modern instrument. This matter of tone goes some way to explaining why Baroque trumpet parts present such problems to modern players, who find it hard to control and soften the brilliant, incisive quality of the shorter B flat trumpet.

Attempts to fill out the gapped harmonic range of the trumpet included a form of slide trumpet. This instrument was different from its medieval forerunner in that instead of the whole instrument moving on the mouthpipe it had a double slide in the loop near to the player which was capable of a short movement and could fill some of the gaps in the compass.

In the nineteenth century, valves were fitted to the traditional coiled post horn – an instrument of conical bore played with a cup mouthpiece – to produce the cornet. The undemanding technique of this high-pitched instrument, resulting both from the use of valves and its wider bore,

1 Detail of mechanism of slide trumpet, **2** a nineteenth-century cornet and **3** valve mechanism of modern trumpet

1

2

3

led to its displacing the trumpet for a time, even in the orchestra. The adoption of valves on the trumpet proper was resisted for a long time by conservative admiration for the old D trumpet. When the valved trumpet did eventually become generally accepted, it bore the marks of its struggle against the cornet. The modern trumpet, as we have mentioned, is pitched much higher than its respected ancestor and it also has a somewhat wider bore; to an eighteenth-century player it would hardly seem to be a trumpet at all.

All the problems which beset the makers faced with the inadequacies of the trumpet and horn compass had no bearing on the trombone. From its invention, in the fifteenth century, it was acoustically perfect. It was unique amongst brass instruments in having a completely chromatic range – from the E below the bass clef in the case of the tenor instrument. But it was also entirely free from all problems of intonation which were met with in the other wind instruments, both wood and brass; and it scored even over the stringed instruments, having only one sound-producing agent, a single column of air, as opposed to the four strings of different thickness, and even different materials, of the violin.

The trombone also has a remarkable range of timbre, from the gentle soft-toned quality admired and cultivated from the Renaissance to the end of the eighteenth-century, to the harsh and menacing sounds which are often heard in the modern orchestra. Given its many qualities we may wonder why it was, that during the period when the need for a chromatic brass instrument was producing the experiments and inventions that we have studied above, the trombone, which was built in alto and soprano sizes, was not used to replace the trumpet. The reasons cannot be defined with confidence, but the following suggest themselves. From the first, it was associated with the music of the Church and was also played in consorts with softer instruments; this in turn bred a tradition of playing which had little in common with the brilliance of the trumpet; the power of the trumpeters'

1 A seventeenth-century trombone. **2** a disassembled modern trombone and **3** detail of decoration on **1**

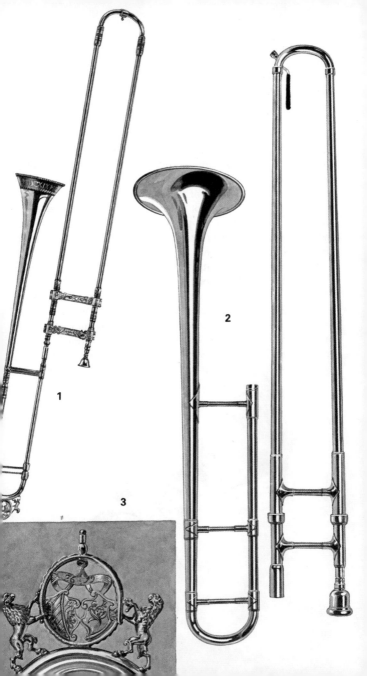

1

2

3

guilds remained strong and can certainly not be discounted; finally, it must be admitted that the trombone does lack a certain brilliance.

Only slight modifications differentiate the modern trombone from the early sackbut. The bell of the modern trombone flares more markedly; the bore, especially in German instruments, is wider and the tone consequently heavier; the slide is somewhat longer allowing a seventh position and, although valves have never been widely popular, modern tenor trombones are frequently fitted with one key that controls a single length of tubing to lower the instrument's pitch by a fourth. This not only extends the range down, but also gives additional slide positions of use in low lying parts, where the slide movements on a standard instrument can be awkward in fast passages.

In the nineteenth century the trombone became a standard member of the military band, and the style of playing changed radically under these new conditions. Morever, as the century progressed, the brass section of such bands was reinforced with the saxhorns and other bass valved instruments. It was in their search for such instruments that the French military authorities turned to the well-known, and also well-connected,

(below) Sydney Bechet, the jazz soprano saxophonist
(opposite left) Modern baritone saxophone. *(right)* Nineteenth-century saxophone

instrument-maker, Adolphe Sax. The saxophone, which has made his name a familiar household word, he invented in Belgium in 1841, and five years later he patented it in France. Its most characteristic shape is that of the lower members of the family, the sopranino and soprano models, being straight and resembling a metal clarinet. Like the clarinet, too, the saxophone has a single beating reed, but unlike the clarinet it has a conical tube; the bore being somewhat wider and the fingerholes larger in diameter. All these features, combined with the fact that the instrument is made of metal and not wood, combine to give it the characteristic nasal quality of tone which has prevented its ever becoming a regular member of the orchestra. Sax built his new instrument in fourteen models consisting of two parallel series of seven instruments each – from sopranino to contrabass – one at orchestral pitch, the other at military band pitch. The saxophone has been used by a number of 'serious' composers, but has made its mark in the swing bands and jazz bands of the 'thirties, and is now firmly established.

The harp

By the beginning of the eighteenth century the harp was still an essentially diatonic instrument with a range of some five octaves. Fitted with a string to each note of the diatonic scale, it was by definition incapable of playing sharps or flats, accidentals which were increasingly called for as composers began to make more use of chromatic harmonies. A 'double' harp is recorded in the early years of the seventeenth century, which was fitted with a second row of strings to give full chromatic range in the middle part of the instrument's compass. This stresses one of the major problems of the harp builder. Since a certain minimum space must be allowed between one string and the next to allow room for the player to pluck with freedom, a harp with a separate string for each note, in the full chromatic range of five octaves, would have to be so large as to be virtually unmanageable. Another early attempt to solve the problem gave the harp three rows of strings, the centre providing the accidentals. It is hardly necessary to emphasize the difficulties of playing an instrument such as this at any speed.

In the 1720s, a Bavarian maker, Simon Hochbrucker of Donauwörth, produced a partial solution that was to provide the basis for all future developments in harp manufacture. His answer was to devise a mechanism which raised the pitch of the strings, and it is improved mechanisms of this type that make up the subsequent history of the concert harp. In the earliest model the string length was shortened by a hook which was operated by a pedal and a tracker action rising through the vertical front pillar. There were seven pedals in all, one for each degree of the scale and raising its pitch a semi-tone in all the octaves. Thus depressing one pedal would raise all the C's on the instrument to C sharp, another would raise all the D's to D sharp, and so on. The main drawbacks of this mechanism were, first, that the hooks which raised the pitch of the string also pulled it out of the vertical alignment, and secondly, the pitch of each string could be raised only a semi-tone. This meant that although more keys were now available to the harpist, the full range of the major and minor keys was not. Makers continued to grapple with the difficulties presented, and the French maker,

Marie Antoinette's harp and detail of the neck of an Érard harp of the 1880s

Georges Cousineau of Paris, improved the earlier mechanism by replacing the hooks with mobile vanes, which pinched the strings and thus shortened their length without pulling them out of alignment.

But as the pedal harp became increasingly used and harpists perfected their technique, the shortcomings of the instrument became increasingly obvious. Some of the most important advances in technique were made by J. B. Krumpholz, the harpist in the orchestra of Prince Esterházy, who came to settle in Paris. There he posed the problems of the harp to the piano maker, Sébastien Érard. From this emerged Érard's double-action harp, with elaborate scrollwork, which he patented in 1810 and which has remained basically unchanged. This model had only seven pedals and an added second fork for each string.

The modern concert harp has a range of about six and a half octaves. It consists of the following principal parts: the pedestal, which not only supports the instrument proper but also carries the pedals; the body, usually made of spruce wood and providing the resonator; the pillar, which both braces the neck and is hollow so as to contain the rods which transmit the motion of the pedals to the action; and the neck, which carries the strings and also the action itself.

Despite the improvement that it represented, the Érard double-action harp was opposed in its country of origin, partly thanks to the influence of F.-J. Naderman, a rival maker of single-action harps, who also, from 1825, was professor of the harp at the Paris *Conservatoire*. But elsewhere it was eagerly taken up and its technique explored and perfected, so that although subsequent attempts have been made to produce a fully chromatic instrument, they have never succeeded in displacing the pedal harp. The most successful of these chromatic harps, with a separate string to each note of the chromatic scale, was produced by the French firm of Pleyel, who solved the problems of space referred to earlier, by crossing the strings diagonally so that the player could pluck them freely above or below the point of their intersection. This instrument was, insofar as it dispensed with pedal action, designed to make the playing of chromatic passages simpler.

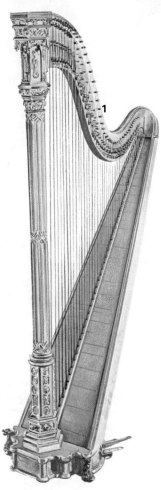

2 Chromatic harp with diagonal stringing

1 French double-action harp

133

The great organ of Ste-Clotilde, Paris, by Cavaillé Col (1862)

The Romantic organ

If only because it is usually built in a church, the organ has generally been associated with ecclesiastical music. But after the last great glories of the north German Baroque Style – faintly echoed in England in the organ concertos of Handel – the music of the Church, and hence of the organ, became increasingly less important. Consequently very few major works were written during the nineteenth century, even though the skill of the makers continued to produce fine instruments.

Although the best Romantic organs had qualities outstanding in their own right, they had nothing in common with the principles of brilliance, contrast and balance of the Baroque organs described earlier. There are a few technical advances, the most obvious being the late, but widespread, adoption of pedalboards in England during the eighteenth century, and the growing importance of the swell mechansim. As we might expect, the Romantic organ was designed to emulate the qualities admired in the new symphony orchestra of the period.

At least from the beginning of the seventeenth century, organ makers named their pipes after the wind instruments then common, and the famous Compenius organ of 1610, for example, is regarded by some researchers as one of the most valuable archives as to the sound expected from early instruments. We have seen how the style of orchestral playing shifted during the eighteenth century from one of marked and largely ungraduated contrasts to one of nuance of instrumental colour and volume dynamic. The mixture stops, so important in the Baroque instrument, were much less prominent in the nineteenth-century organ, the coupler mechanism which allows the player to combine stops from different manuals was more often used, and frequent and subtle changes of registration – the term for the selection and combination of stops by the player – were the order of the day. Above all, the swell box, which had from the eighteenth century allowed for gradual swelling and diminution of volume, came to the fore. (The department known as the swell organ was enclosed

Sunday morning service on the New York to San Francisco Pullman car, a harmonium accompanies the singing

Five-manual console of the new organ at Notre-Dame Cathedral, Paris

by louvred doors, which could be gradually opened or closed by the operation of a foot pedal). The interest in graduated dynamics also affected the design of stops, the pipes being graded from loud to soft, so that, drawing on such successive graduated stops, the organist could build up to massive *crescendos*. Such effects, common enough in the orchestral music of the day, were virtually unknown to the Baroque organ style, in which the effective balancing of the contrasting parts of the contrapuntal structure depended on the stops being of roughly equal power.

The expressive qualities of the Romantic organ, while making it unsuitable for performances of Bach, made it an ideal instrument for the performance of arrangements of orchestral music; a function not to be underestimated for a society without the gramophone or radio. Moreover, major works which were written for the organ by composers such as Liszt and Franck reveal the truly fine music which it could produce.

The invention of the pneumatic action by an Englishman, Joseph Booth of Wakefield, in the 1820s, revolutionized the possibilities of the organ builder. The aim was to lighten the touch of the instrument and this was achieved by making the action of the keys control, not the pallets under the pipes, but valves which operated small bellows that opened the pallets. After this, inhibitions on size – determined by the heavy key-work and action of the old trackers – were removed, and when the twentieth century introduced electric circuitry as the means of transmission between key and bellows, all restraint could be thrown aside. Both in Europe and America, organs of immense proportions, sometimes with as many as two hundred stops, were built in concert halls and congress centres. Impressive in their dimensions, but not always in their musical qualities, these monsters were soon to provoke a reaction.

Old organs are now being extensively used for recordings and broadcasts, while modern builders are constructing instruments capable of the full range of both the Baroque and the Romantic organ. One of the first reactions to the mammoth instruments was the so-called 'Praetorius organ', built in 1921 by the German firm of Walcker, for the Musicological Institute in Freiburg. Since that time a number of all-purpose organs, with complete Baroque sections, have been built – some of the finest in America, and one of the handsomest in the Festival Hall, London.

The Festival Hall organ, London

(left) Nineteenth-century hand-tuned kettledrum and *(right)* modern machine drum

Percussion instruments
The drums

Of all the percussion instruments the kettledrums are the most romantic, both in their history and their mode of playing. Among the most exciting sights are the spectacular flourishes of the horse drummer in the Household Cavalry, when the sovereign's escort of the Queen of England is in procession. It was from the mounted bands of the Turkish army that Europe adapted the large kettledrums during the fifteenth century, and from the reign of Henry VIII they were firmly established in English and Continental military music. In view of the veneration accorded the drums in primitive societies, it is of great interest to trace the history of the kettledrum in the West. From the beginning it was the preserve of royalty and this tradition was emphasized in England for a few years after the Restoration, when only the band of the Household Cavalry was permitted a pair of drums. All over

Europe the drummers were joined with the trumpeters to form the most privileged and respected groups in the world of professional music, and their characteristic tunes and rhythms were jealously guarded. During the later part of the seventeenth century, composers began to introduce these effects into their ceremonial or dramatic music, and from the time of Bach and Handel the kettledrums (sometimes also known in English by their Italian name, *timpani*) were regular members of the orchestra.

For the most part they were tuned to the dominant and tonic notes of the key of the music, and it was not until the symphonies of Beethoven, who sometimes tuned his drums in octaves and also made much effective use of the drum roll, that their possibilities began to be fully explored. The nineteenth century was the age of experiment with the orchestra, and the most important single figure in every aspect of orchestration was the French composer, Hector

The horse drummer of the Household Cavalry

Berlioz. From his time the traditional pair of drums was increased to three, and occasionally he wrote parts which required two timpanists – each controlling two or three drums – who were required to play chords by rolling on two differently tuned drums. Berlioz also made a revolutionary change in the sound of the kettledrum in the orchestra by demanding soft-headed sticks for certain parts.

The kettledrum is an essentially simple structure, consisting of a deep copper bowl (the 'kettle'), between two foot and two foot six inches (75 centimetres) in diameter, over which is stretched a 'head' of calf vellum, or, more commonly now, of plastic. This is lapped over a hoop which circles the outer rim of the drum and the vellum can be tightened, and its pitch raised, by forcing this hoop down by means of hand-operated screws or some form of mechanism. The range of such a drum covers an interval of a fourth and the range of a complete set of different-sized drums is very rarely more than a tenth – from the E flat below the bass staff to the G a tenth above it. But, although limited in range, the drumhead can be exactly tuned and a good ear is essential for the timpanist, who may have to make changes of tuning while the orchestra is playing in a different key from the one for which he is preparing the drums.

A military side drum

From the late nineteenth century, models of machine drum have been produced; in conjunction with a plastic head, which is free from the variations induced in natural vellum by changes in temperature or humidity, they give very reliable tunings which can, if necessary, be finely tuned with hand screws. More interesting, perhaps, than the rapid tuning that it makes possible, is the fact that the machine drum opens up the possibility of a *glissando* effect on the drums, the player gradually slackening or tightening the head as he plays a roll.

Over the four centuries of its development in the West, the kettledrum has been subject to certain refinements. The head often has become a thinner vellum than on the cavalry instrument and the tone quality has been modified by the

(left) A 'battery' of drums and percussion effects. *(right)* Cymbals

introduction of various types of soft-headed sticks in place of the wooden ones used in the orchestra up to the time of Beethoven and Berlioz.

As the kettledrum began its career in the cavalry regiments, so the side drum was for long only to be heard in the marching bands of the infantry. Of medieval European antecedents, it is now constructed in the form of a fairly shallow metal shell, about twelve inches (30 centimetres) in diameter, with heads across top and bottom. The bottom head is usually fitted with a 'ribbon' of wires which can be brought against it to rattle when the drum is struck. It is these 'snares' that produce the characteristic sound of the side drum, though in the orchestra it may also be played without them. Somewhat larger is the tenor drum, primarily a military instrument, though also used in various forms in the jazz battery, along with the side drums which here are often played with wire brushes, and in the orchestra. The last of the untuned drums in common orchestral use is the bass drum. Like the *timpani* it is also of Turkish origin and, along with the large Turkish cymbals and the triangle, was introduced into the European concert hall in the later eighteenth century, when this 'Turkish' or 'Janissary' music enjoyed a certain fashion. In the orchestra the bass drum may have one or two heads and is usually about three feet (90 centimetres) in diameter. In the jazz band it is somewhat smaller and is often played with a felt-covered stick operated by a foot pedal.

The cymbals

Among the most dramatic sights that the orchestra has to offer is the cymbal clash. These large Turkish instruments are quite different from the small tuned finger cymbals of Antiquity – the so-called 'ancient cymbals'. They can, however, produce a number of other effects, and often in the orchestra as in the jazz band, a single cymbal suspended on a pillar is played with wooden or felt-covered sticks. The tone quality of the cymbals is determined by the exact proportions of metals used in producing the alloy from which they are made – roughly eight parts of copper to two parts of tin. Some of the finest cymbals are made by a family of Armenian manufacturers, who have preserved the secret formula of their alloy for some three centuries.

The xylophone

The xylophone, a form of which was used in certain European folk traditions, consists of a series of tuned wooden bars, giving a chromatic range of about three and a half to four octaves and played with hard-headed sticks. The *glockenspiel* ('bell

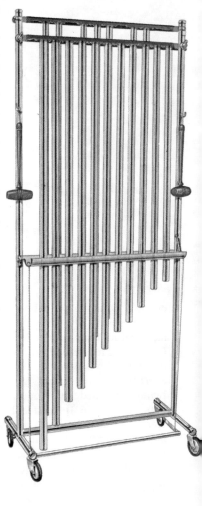

(opposite) A *glockenspiel*.
(above) Orchestral tubular bells

143

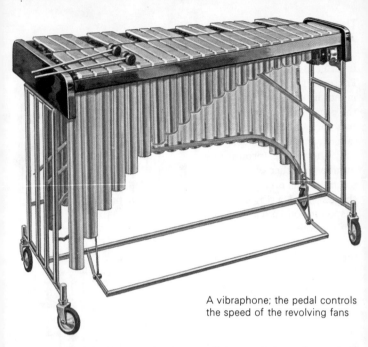

A vibraphone; the pedal controls the speed of the revolving fans

chime'), which is probably an offshoot of the military bell lyre, is essentially the same instrument, but is fitted with metal rather than wooden keys. In 1935 William F. Ludwig of Chicago added resonators. In a slightly modified form, and fitted with a keyboard, the *glockenspiel* gave birth to the *celesta*. This instrument is in the form of a small upright piano, invented by Auguste Mustel of Paris, which he patented in 1886. It has steel bars suspended over box-shaped wooden resonators and is struck by piano hammers. The *marimba*, derived from Indonesian and African instruments, is a deep-toned xylophone with tubular metal resonators under the keys, and it, in turn, has been modified to produce the vibraphone. This instrument, which has found a number of jazz virtuosi, is a metal-keyed *marimba*, which is usually played with soft-headed sticks and fitted with a metal fan at the top of each of the tubular resonators; the fans, operated by an electric motor, can be made to revolve at varying speeds, and the turbulence they set up in the air column impart a more or less rapid *vibrato* to the tone.

Other types of instrument belonging to the xylophone family are the *xyleuphone*; this is a keyed xylophone invented by Culmbach of Heilbron in about 1835 and is worked by wind pressure supplied by bellows. A friction xylophone invented by another German – Uthe of Sangerhausen – in about 1808, is called the *xylosistron*. It consists of a set of graduated wooden bars laid horizontally and stroked by the player's rosin-coated gloves.

In the twentieth century, Western ears have become used to an infinitely larger range of percussive sounds than ever before. The bongo drums of South America, the wooden 'cowbell' and Chinese temple block, the sharp report of a wooden clapper – known as a 'whip', are only some of the many new sounds to be heard in jazz or modern orchestral music. A more important group, however, is that of the fixed-note percussion instruments, long familiar in the music of the Indonesian *gamelan*, but only heard in European 'art' music over the last hundred years.

Type of African *marimba* with keys and resonators

POPULAR INSTRUMENTS

There seems little doubt that it was the Chinese *sheng* which, becoming known in Europe during the eighteenth-century, encouraged the experiments with free reeds being made in early nineteenth-century Europe. It also has been suggested that these might have originated in attempts to modify and improve the plucked metal 'reed' instrument, long known in Europe as the Jew's-harp. One of the most familiar of these instruments was the concertina, perfected by Sir Charles Wheatstone during the 1830s. The original model, at treble pitch, had a range of about four octaves; since then, larger sizes have been built. The wind is supplied by a hand-operated expandable hexagonal bellows; the reeds are in the heads at either end. There are two reeds to each note and they are controlled by stop finger buttons in the casing of the heads.

But the concertina was not the first such instrument in the field nor did it, despite considerable popularity in the hands of virtuosi during the last century, prove the most long-lasting. In the twentieth century easily the most popular of the free-reed instruments has been the accordion. It was invented in Germany during the 1820s, and soon became such a popular domestic instrument that despite the patent, it was freely copied by other makers who did little but change the name. The nineteenth-century accordion was fitted with brass reeds which were neither powerful nor stable enough for large concert hall use, but when in the early years of this century makers began to use steel reeds, the popularity of the instrument grew still further. The instrument in its most developed form is large. The melody reeds are controlled by a piano-like keyboard held against the body of the player and are played with the fingers of the right hand. The left hand operates an impressive number of buttons, which control reeds to provide a number of bass notes, while others bring a variety of three-note chords into play.

Last among the members of the free-reed family to be treated are the smallest – the mouth-blown harmonica, and the largest – the bellows-blown harmonium. Like all other members of the group, the pitch of the notes is determined by the length and thickness of the metal reeds. The harmonium –

(above) A mouth organ. *(centre)* This early accordion was made in 1829. *(below)* A modern accordian

invented by a Frenchman, Alexandre-François Debain of Paris, in 1840 – gained tremendous popularity as a domestic instrument and for the accompaniment of the singing in small churches; it has also been used occasionally by major composers. The tendency to monotony of tone quality can be corrected by the use of a number of stops of different timbres and also of a device for swelling the volume of sound. The harmonica – most closely related to the Chinese precursor of the family – has earned the highest place in the concert repertoire and is now built in a full range of sizes, from treble to bass.

For most of their comparatively short history, the free-reed instruments have found their greatest use in the home, and it was here that the harmonium was most cultivated. However, in the twentieth century this small drawing-room 'organ' is increasingly losing ground to the electronic organ, of which the most successful and widely-known models are probably those of the Hammond Company of America. The sound is generated by oscillations of electric circuits and most makers aim to imitate, though with less than complete success, the sounds of the natural pipe organ.

Undoubtedly the most familiar of all electric instruments is the electric guitar. In its most usual form it consists of a

(above) A ukelele
(below) A modern banjo

frame to carry the strings, whose vibrations are directly converted into electric impulses and then amplified; less commonly the sounds of a traditional guitar may be amplified on the principle of the megaphone.

Other fretted instruments are the 'Hawaiian' electric guitar, in which the strings are stopped by a metal bar and made to slide along the strings by the player's left hand, the ukelele (U.S. ukulele) – a diminutive cousin of the Spanish guitar, and the banjo. Known since the beginning of the eighteenth century, this last instrument was brought to America by black African slaves who called it the *banjar*. In its original form it had four gut strings, was hand plucked and derived its characteristic shape from its long neck and the unique form of its body. This may most simply be described as an open-ended tambourine, covered on one side by a vellum head and with the other side left open. During the nineteenth century the banjo became the preferred instrument of the 'minstrel' shows, but it has recovered its dignity as a serious musical instrument during this century in the hands of a small number of jazz musicians.

A Hawaiian guitar

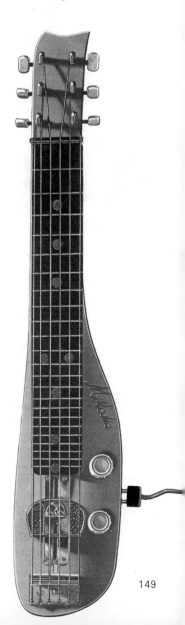

An eighteenth-century automaton. *(opposite)* A musical box and diagram showing the mechanism

MUSICAL AUTOMATA

Instruments played by mechanical means are as old as Classical Antiquity. A Greek writer of ancient Alexandria describes a *hydraulis* organ that was played by a mechanism driven by a windmill. From the invention of clockwork movements in the later Middle Ages, their machinery was applied not only to ringing the chimes of the clock itself but also to independent musical instruments, and a remarkable example of a mechanical carillon built in Delft in the 1560s is still used. The heart of the mechanism is a massive copper drum pierced with thousands of holes into which the carilloneur fits metal pins that operate a trip mechanism on the frame, to activate the strikers that sound the bells. As the drum slowly revolves the pins engage, and it is their exact placing in the drum that decides which bells are rung and the frequency with which they are struck. This principle was applied in late eighteenth-century Switzerland to the musical box.

During the eighteenth century automata of all kinds were

produced, ranging from dolls that performed on toy harpsichords to musical machines that played a band of wind instruments. At times the noble organ itself had automatic effects fitted to it, such as drums beaten with sticks on a trip mechanism, but the most familiar to the modern eye is the Polyphon. This was the true forerunner of the modern juke box, being set up in public places and playing a tune for a penny in the slot. The instrument was provided with a number of pierced and pinned metal discs that plucked the teeth of the metal comb, and was fitted with an automatic changer.

Automata are a fascinating study in their own right, despite the brief mention that they necessarily receive here. However, it should be remembered that even Mozart wrote his magnificent *Fantasia* for a mechanical organ, and Beethoven wrote his rather less magnificent *Battle Symphony* for the *panharmonicon*, invented by Johann Nepomuk Mältzel, and designed to perform mechanically a battery of instruments reproducing virtually the full range of the orchestra.

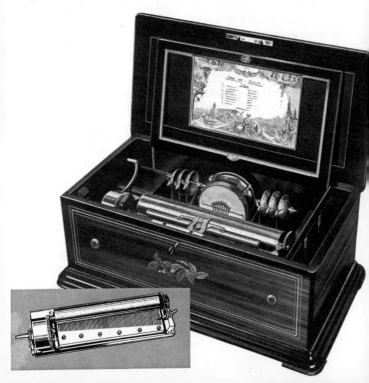

NEW DIRECTIONS

Throughout history instruments have been invented, discarded or modified according not only to fashion, but to the musical requirements of composers and performers. Improvements have sometimes been prompted by the new demands made by a new generation of composers. Sometimes the inventor's ingenuity has thrown up an instrument that has inspired the composer. Such was the case with the clarinet and, above all, the piano. Both were invented in the early eighteenth century and both anticipated the development of music by several decades, but awaited the genius of Mozart to be fully revealed.

The invention of new instruments never ceases; the saxophone, the vibraphone, the electric guitar have all found an important place in different regions of the world of music. The application of electricity to music-making has produced a number of startling new instruments that astonish the eye with their unfamiliar appearance and the ear by their remarkable new sounds. Most generally accepted of these to date has been the *ondes martenot*; it generates sound from the interference patterns set up between a fixed and variable radio frequency oscillator. Like the *ondes martenot*, the *Theremin*, also named after its maker, is a melodic instrument generating sound by the interaction of fixed and variable oscillators. Both these instruments date from the 1920s. More recent experimentors have achieved many new and remarkable effects with the aid of electricity, while others have dispensed with it and returned to the world of natural resonances. One group of French designers have demonstrated an instrument working on the principle of the glass harmonica, but using vertical glass rods of different lengths rather than drinking glasses. These, and many other experimental instrumental instruments, however, can only be referred to briefly in this book.

It has been starkly prophesied that in the not so distant future the musician and composer will be able to transmit the electrical impulses themselves directly to the brain patterns of their audience and that the only 'musical instrument' of the future will be an electrode taped to the listener's forearm. Yet even when that day is reached, we shall still be men, and as men will still be susceptible to the charms of music, however they reach us.

A polyphon — the 'juke-box' of the nineteenth century

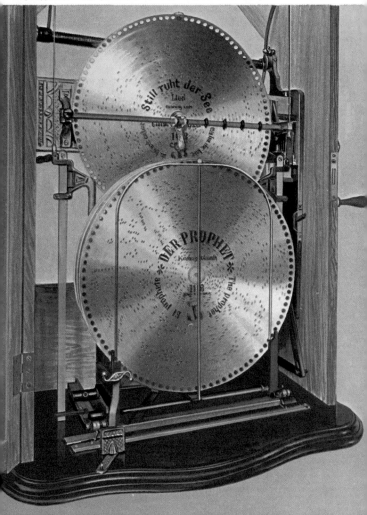

GLOSSARY

Action, general term for the mechanism of keyboard instruments such as the piano, harpsichord or organ

Belly, top surface of the sound-box of a stringed instrument; also sometimes called the 'table'

Body, the sound-box of a stringed instrument

Bore, precisely the inside diameter of a tube, but sometimes loosely used of the tube itself. Thus the terms 'conical' or 'cylindrical' bore are commonly used to describe a tube cylindrical or conical in shape

Bell, refers not only to the musical instruments but also to the widely flaring part of the tube of a wind instrument. The French term *'pavillon'* is also but rarely used in English

Bourdon, term used of a continuous bass note held beneath a melody line; in this sense it has the same meaning as 'drone'. It may also refer to any low-pitched note and in this sense is used of certain types of organ stop

Bridge, wooden bar or structure on a stringed instrument over which the string passes or to which it is anchored and which defines its sounding length. Bridges are of two main kinds: a pressure bridge as on the violin, held in place by the pressure of the strings that pass over it; and a tension bridge, attached to the belly of the instrument, to which the strings are tied, as on a guitar

Chromatic scale, one using all the semi-tones in the octave. An instrument with a chromatic compass can sound all the notes at the interval of a semi-tone from one another between two specified limits

Compass, the range of notes that can be sounded by any instrument

Conical bore or **tube,** certain wind instruments have tubes in the shape of an extended cone. In the case of brass instruments this affects the tone; in the case of woodwind instruments it affects the overblowing of notes above the natural compass

Cylindrical bore or **tube,** wind instruments with this type of tube are different in tone quality from those with a conical tube; woodwind instruments overblow different harmonics

Diatonic scale, scale of tone and semi-tone intervals with the semi-tones between the third and fourth and the seventh and eighth degrees

Drone, *see* **Bourdon**

Harmonic series, series of notes that can be derived from a vibrating string or column of air; they ascend according to mathematical ratios and the first steps are the octave, the fifth above it, the fourth above that, then a major third, then a minor third. Not all the upper intervals correspond exactly to those of the diatonic scale but the higher the harmonics the closer they lie together, so that the upper range of the series on brass instruments, such as the natural trumpet, can be used melodically

Nut, 1) bridge at the top of the neck of the violin 2)

movable block at the end of a violin bow to which is attached the ribbon of the hair

Overblow, to blow a wood-wind instrument so that each basic fingering yields another higher note; in general these higher notes are an octave above the bass note but in the clarinet – a single reed instrument with a cylindrical tube – they are a twelfth higher

Plectrum, small piece of wood, leather or plastic used to pluck the stings of such instruments as the guitar

Transposing instrument, one for which the composer writes the part at a pitch to suit the player in reading the fingering rather than at the pitch at which the notes actually sound

BOOKS TO READ

Musical Instruments and their Symbolism in Western Art by E. Winternitz. Faber and Faber, London 1967.

Musical Instruments of the Western World by E. Winternitz. Thames and Hudson, London, 1967.

Musical Instruments: A Comprehensive Dictionary by Sybil Marcuse. Country Life, London, 1966.

Musical Instruments in Art and History by R. Bragard and F. J. de Hen. Barrie and Rockliff, London, 1968.

Musical Instruments through the Ages edited by Anthony Baines. Faber and Faber, London, 1966.

PLACES TO VISIT

In Britain

Victoria & Albert Museum, London
Fenton House, Hampstead, London (Benton-Fletcher Collection)
Royal College of Music, London (Donaldson Collection)
Horniman Museum, London
Birmingham School of Music, Birmingham
Royal Manchester College of Music, Manchester
The Scottish National Academy, Glasgow
Museum of Music and Musical Instruments, Edinburgh University
City Museum & Art Gallery, Dundee, Scotland

In America

Museum of Music, Scarsdale, New York
Musical Museum, Deansboro, New York
Metropolitan Museum of Art, New York
Symphony Hall, Boston (Casadesus Collection)
Museum of Fine Arts, Boston
University of Michigan (Stearns Collection)
Edison Institute, Dearborn (Chickering Collection)
Collection of Musical Instruments, Yale University

INDEX

SOME OTHER TITLES IN THIS SERIES